# An Appetite for Change?

# An Appetite for Change?

Are Governments, Society and Farmers willing to make the changes that are now necessary to ensure the wellbeing of future generations?

PHILIP RICHARDSON
May 2019

THE CHOIR PRESS

First published in the United Kingdom in 2019 by
The Choir Press


ISBN 978-1-78963-074-9

# Contents

# Introduction

'The greatest possible irony would be if in our endless quest to fill our lives with comfort and happiness, we created a world that had neither.'

*Bill Bryson (At Home: a short history of private life)[1]*

In a wide ranging book covering topics as diverse as architecture and epidemics Bill Bryson, who for some years was a near neighbour, ends his book expressing concerns about human over exploitation of the Earth's resources. In the quotation above I omitted his final sentence, which is, '*But that, of course would be another book.*' I suspect to cover the topic adequately would need many books, and this short book of mine is but a small contribution.

For much of my adult life I have driven my family mad by cutting out news stories and articles, (often before they have read them), from newspapers, magazines, and even books, on topics which I found thought provoking. The cuttings would pile up on my desk in no particular order until, every year or two, I would go through them, culling those no longer interesting to me and arranging the others into piles, by subject, for future reference, should I ever need to remind myself of their content.

Almost twenty years ago the topic piles that remained largely reflected my growing concerns over the future trajectory for farming and food, and growing disquiet over climate change and human destruction of the environment. When I retired I decided to spend some time getting more up to speed on these topics, with particular emphasis on their global nature. I already had a pretty good knowledge of UK agriculture and associated environmental and political debates, in which I was often personally involved during my working life, as a member of various committees and groups both nationally and locally. So I went back to University to study climate change and international development, there discovering a whole new world of academic literature, very different in quantity and subject matter from that which I had encountered during my first degree in agriculture in the 1960's.

That started me on a journey of personal discovery, although at that stage I had no intention of committing myself to print. This book has had a long gestation of almost a decade. In that time research has moved on apace; challenges and potential solutions have been refined. At the outset the simple question in my mind was 'how can we adequately feed the hugely bigger world population expected by the mid 21st century?' Innovation in farming techniques was evidently slowing down. Was this a temporary phenomenon or were we facing a Malthusian domesday scenario? New scientific techniques to lift yields of crops and increase the efficiency of animal production were beginning to appear. Frequently the science was criticised by environmentalists who persuaded some governments to stop its commercialisation. Innovation with a 'green' face was surely the way forward? Only somewhat later in my journey did the penny drop that the parallel concerns of rising ill health resulting, primarily, from poor modern dietary habits, were closely linked to all the other concerns over food and the environment. Even now, in 2019, there is little widespread appreciation of this linkage from the general public or in government.

There is a vast range of literature available on all of the topics in this book, but most limits itself to one topic, or is academic and not easily accessible to the public at large. Little of the academic literature deals with practical governmental problems and responsibilities, and I am not aware of any source which attempts to paint a global picture of the issues from a farmers perspective.

Throughout the text, which I hope is relatively easily understood, I have referenced sources for those readers who wish to look in more depth at particular topics. The book is deliberately short, in the hope that it will be read in its entirety, because the message I want to convey most strongly is the need for broad based understanding of complex but interlinked issues as a basis for moving forward successfully to meet very big challenges. I am critical, from time to time, of political and corporate leaders, but as I often say, when others also criticise, but do nothing themselves that, 'we get what we deserve'.

In writing this book over such a long period I found myself swinging wildly from periods of optimism that my successors will be able to share the fortunate life that has been granted to me, to other times of deep pessimism that necessary actions and agreements will not be made in time to prevent catastrophe. There are already plenty of 'domesday merchants' who have written apocalyptic books, but my feeling is that readers tend to switch off when confronted with too much bad news. I would rather be optimistic that my grandchildrens generation will be more sensible than my generation has been.

Philip Richardson

May 2019

# Summary

Over the next few decades the world faces several unprecedented challenges. Top of the list is climate change, but it interacts in complex ways with a host of other very significant global issues. Central to many of these issues is agriculture. We need farms to produce our food, but farming and its associated industry sectors, from fertiliser manufacture to fast food companies, make massive demands on global resources such as freshwater and soil. This agri-food complex is a major driver of climate change as well as the cause of huge worldwide environmental degradation and species loss. Can the industry match food supply to increasing demand from a rising world population with a growing taste for animal protein based diets? The production of meat and milk uses up scarce land and water resources and increases greenhouse gas emissions which cause climate change. Changing climate is likely to reduce average agricultural yields and threatens stability of supply from season to season. The poorest nations on earth are set to suffer the worst consequences, having less capacity to cope with change and because the poor generally live in parts of the world where climate change is more destructive. In these regions the priorities must be to raise food production and try to ensure what is produced reaches those who are most in need. In other regions, where food supplies are currently more than adequate, there is evidence that poor quality diets are seriously affecting health. Obesity is now more widespread in the world than hunger or malnutrition, and its associated chronic medical conditions consume an increasing proportion of healthcare budgets. Antibiotic resistance poses a further threat to human health and some farm practices are partially held to blame.

In the developed world most political consideration has centred on how we can increase agricultural productivity without further damaging the environment. The most generally acknowledged way to achieve this is called 'sustainable intensification' but it is the subject of much controversy between environmentalists and agriculturalists. Some useful scientific and technical innovations are hampered by public concern over the risk of potentially damaging consequences. Widespread ignorance and suspicion of science also feeds into complacency about climate change. Simpler concepts, such as reducing food waste, improving dietary choices and encouraging healthy lifestyles are now on the political agenda, but there is little 'joined up' policy-making to bring all of these issues together. Rising influence of lobbyists and single-issue pressure groups is not particularly helpful. The public at large, as well as scientists, captains of industry and politicians need a broader understanding of the issues and of the links between them.

Our economic system encourages a continually rising level of consumption whilst failing to recognise that earths' resources are limited. It also fails to assign the true cost of consequential damage done to the environment through over-exploitation or pollution. For instance, the benefits of reducing emissions of greenhouse gases are global, while the costs of new technologies to reduce them are local – providing an incentive to individuals and governments to 'free-ride', in the hope that others will bear the costs. Similarly, the high cost of ill health to individuals and to healthcare budgets is rarely met by those whose products contribute to the problems. Modern capitalism is evidently in urgent need of fundamental reform to retain the progressive power of the 'market' but re-direct it to reflect 'true costs'.

Tackling the global challenges of climate change and environmental destruction requires international cooperation on an unprecedented scale. Belief in the power of technological innovation to solve our problems is widely used as an excuse for not making uncomfortable and unpopular lifestyle changes now. Understanding of the broader range of connected issues by a well informed public can pressure politicians to act. A poorly informed public will disregard the warning signs and be hostile to change. The other big driver for inaction is concern that other nations will not pull their weight. The world needs leadership of the highest order to communicate what is needed and to achieve the necessary level of international cooperation and coordination. Such leadership is not widely evident in the world of 2019. Without widespread cooperation unilateral actions by individual countries will be insufficient to meet the scale of response required, although some countries such as the UK could be beacons for others to follow. In order to remain in power most democratically elected politicians give great weight to short term issues, but the challenges highlighted in this book require long term and consistent policies, over much more than one electoral cycle, to change entrenched attitudes and lifestyles. In the private sector companies should not exist simply to enrich their shareholders.

They should also embrace appropriate social responsibility for the world in which they operate. Particular responsibility falls on multi-national food and agricultural companies which can command great influence over consumers and impose their will on farmers. Even with a generally supportive public and inspirational leaders in politics and industry, achieving what is required will be far from easy. It will be made all the more difficult because of self interest, greed, rampant corruption and venality, all of which plague too many modern societies.

Written by a farmer this book looks at the challenges from a practical viewpoint. It concludes that the mass of individual farming businesses worldwide will react to whatever economic and political actions are imposed upon them, but many will not be passive bystanders. They will be in the frontline taking practical decisions to cope with the effects of climate change, reacting to calls to modify what people eat and to managing the farm environment. They will need access to innovative science and new ways of working. They will also need incentivisation, technical and financial support, and regulation to steer their progress. Poor farmers in less wealthy countries often cannot afford to take any risks and may, therefore, resist pressure to change. Priorities there may include greater investment in basic infrastructure such as roads, storage facilities and markets, not forgetting the importance of strong and equitable rule of law. There is no simple, 'one size fits all' solution. Actions should reflect local conditions and local needs ,and above all should be practical in addressing complex issues holistically and sympathetically. Volatility in yields and product prices together with political uncertainty are all bad for farmers, bad for business and ultimately bad for humanity.

The following chapters examine in turn issues of population, climate change, water, soil, technology, environment, waste and diet and health, before reviewing the structure of farming and the wider agri-food complex. The final section puts all of these matters in political, economic and social context and speculates on the difficulties and the opportunities in meeting the challenges. The book takes a global perspective, although, inevitably, because it is written by a UK farmer, a significant proportion of the text derives from this experience.

The time for taking substantive action is short, chiefly because both social change and the adoption of technical innovation happen slowly, over generations, not years. Climate change has been known about for 40 years, but, so far, our global response has been woefully inadequate. We continue to destroy the natural environment, and show little urgency in facing up to looming crises over freshwater supplies, degradation of soils, or pollution of the oceans. Our insatiable appetite to consume the limited resources of our planet at an ever increasing rate shows no sign of abating. Our collective inaction raises questions of morality and of our duty to the generations to come. Our short term desire for ever increasing economic prosperity is challenged by the reality that life for our children will be more uncomfortable if we fail to take tough decisions now.

# Foreword
# An Appetite for Change?

'Live as though you'll die tomorrow, but farm as though you'll live forever.'

*(traditional farming proverb)*

Throughout my forty year career as a commercial farmer in East Anglia I was conscious of this traditional saying. My forebears knew if they cared properly for their land it would continue to feed them and their successors. If they ran down its fertility for short-term gain, they, or their sons and daughters would later reap poor harvests and hard times. It was understood too, in the context of the vulnerability of the wider environment to human interference, by early peoples such as the Australian Aboriginals, whose reverence for their land is reflected in their art and customs. Such under-standing is also reflected in a saying ascribed to the Cree tribe of North American Indians, '*When the last tree is cut down, the last fish eaten and the last stream poisoned, you will realize that you cannot eat money*'. Farmers where I come from recognize this in the word 'stewardship', implying the duty to understand and care for the assets under one's control for the wider long-term good.

The concept of 'stewardship' is embraced by most farmers, but putting it into practice is not so easy. What does it really mean? Does it suggest that some actions taken by farmers are short-sighted, or that the use of particu-lar technologies with potentially harmful effects over the longer term, should be discouraged? In a highly competitive business environment, with low, or non-existent profit margins, should farmers sacrifice their long-term prospects for short-term survival? Do most farmers really have a choice in what they grow, or are they effectively forced to farm in particular ways by the pressure of the 'market' and the need to make a reasonable living? For subsistence farmers in less developed countries that choice may be between survival and starvation. How much do we really understand what good stewardship involves? When I first began farming the industry was in the early stages of a technological and scientific revolution, which transformed the choice and availability of food to consumers from the post war austerity and rationing of the '50's to the cornucopia we enjoy in developed countries today. Food expenditure as a proportion of family income has fallen dramatically over the same period.

But there have been warning signs, suggesting that current consumer lifestyles are not sustainable. Farmers have discovered that yield improvements are increasingly hard to achieve, despite enormous scientific advances in plant and animal breeding and sophisticated chemical antidotes to diseases and pests. Soils are less easy to work even though machinery has become more sophisticated. Many of the birds and wildflowers we used to see regularly are now rare, or have disappeared altogether. If we look beyond our own 'backyard' we find such observations multiplied across the world. As this book reached a conclusion the Intergovernmental Science-Policy Platform on Biodiversity and Ecosystem Services (IPBES)[1] published its first report since 2005. It confirmed that *'nature is declining globally at rates unprecedented in human history.'*

Conservationists claim we are in a new era, the 'Anthropocene', where nature, as a whole is severely affected by the huge influence of one species – humans. There are now so many of us, and we use so much of the limited resources of the planet, that we risk long-term catastrophe for the sake of short-term gain. They question the way our entire economic system drives exploitation of resources with no regard to long term consequences. Farming will play a central role in how society comes to terms with the challenges we all now face.

Since the industrial revolution, which began in England in the eighteenth century, we have witnessed exponential growth in human populations associated with continual growth in consumption of an increasing range of goods, such that we have come to take economic growth for granted. As Mervyn King, Governor of the Bank of England 2003-2013, writes in his book *'The End of Alchemy'*[2] (2016), *growth of productivity resulted from specialization in particular tasks. This went hand in hand with an increased role for money and banks to allow the exchange of 'the fruits of one's labour for an ever wider variety of goods produced by other specialists'.*

Modern capitalism fails to take into account what scientists term the 'commons' – that is the elements which contribute to our lifestyles, but which 'belong to everyone and no-one'. These includes the open oceans, the air we breathe and the vast expanse of wilderness in the world, together with its flora and fauna, which effectively belongs to no-one, or is beyond effective jurisdiction of capable Government. Students of history will recall the many periods of 'enclosure' in England between the sixteenth and nineteenth centuries, when acquisitive landlords fenced in land previously used 'in common' by society as a whole. They claimed that single ownership provided an incentive to improve the productivity of the land and stopped previous over exploitation and abuse. There are striking parallels between irresponsible treatment of common and the current over-exploitation of fish resources in the open oceans and the relative freedom we all have to use and abuse the atmosphere, resulting in excessive emissions of greenhouse gases, responsible for changing our climate, or pollutants from vehicles harming our childrens lungs.

While politicians continue to argue over the right to ownership by the many and not by the few, modern civilisations have generally proved themselves incapable of emulating the native American example, instanced at the start of this chapter, of respect for nature and an absence of personal property rights. Instead, industrialised societies have largely concluded that public ownership is often inefficient, lacking innovation and very far from the idealised utopia of joint ownership and joint responsibility which so entrances some political thinking.

Inevitably, 'stewardship of the commons' necessitates a global view of the effects of the human species on the planet. The emissions of carbon dioxide, nitrous oxide and methane that result from my farming operations cannot be contained within the farm boundary. They become part of the atmosphere circulating our planet, adding to the emissions from every other farm, every other business, home or vehicle in the world. Many books and academic articles have been written about the challenges presented by climate change, and many world leaders have, at last, woken up to the need to respond, although such response already looks to many experts in the field as being too little, too late.

Amongst the general public, and within the farming community too, there is a dearth of knowledge on this and associated problems, and in particular, a lack of appreciation of their global nature. Farmers are in the frontline of environmental and climate change and will be the primary target of much political and social change in coming decades. Politicians may set the strategic framework for agriculture, and consumers may apply economic and social pressures, but it is farmers who must translate these signals into practice. But farmers and the food industry are often blinkered in their approach to what needs to be done. Partly this is due to lack of knowledge or appreciation of the global framework within which future policies must be framed. This book aims to give an overview of the current and future challenges in which the agriculture and food industries must play a major role.

So far most government proposals to meet the challenges are partial, inward looking and unambitious. There is no overall internationally agreed strategy framework for environmental protection. The climate change accord reached in Paris in 2015 faces huge political hurdles. Massively important issues of diet and health are often not linked to agriculture and food policy by politicians, and many in the food industry prefer not to talk about them. Some change, however, is in the air. As I approached the end of writing this book I received a copy of the Lancet Commission Report [3], which calls for international concerted action to link actions which address all of these issues simultaneously.

A true long-term strategy needs to be radical if it is to be effective. Radicalism is difficult to achieve within a democracy without adequate understanding of the necessity for action by a broad section of the public. There is an old African saying; '*If you want to go quickly, go alone; if you want to go far, go together*'. The difficulty is that most of the radical solutions, and even the less radical ones, such as bringing new improved crops to market on a wide scale, have a long lead time, (perhaps 25 years or more from variety development to widespread use as a food product). Stimulating significant dietary change is similarly difficult and slow.

But we don't have much time. Climate change is happening now, and more quickly than originally thought. It is already causing extreme and unpredictable weather patterns, droughts, floods, sea level rise and uncertain harvests in many parts of the world. Global population is rising fast. With no change in current dietary trends the worlds' farmers will probably need to raise total food production by more than half as much again as they produce now. Logically that production should largely take place where it is most needed – where populations are growing, and where agriculture and food technologies are still poorly developed. Otherwise the economies of these countries will never grow, and the world will see more poverty and hunger, and their inevitable partners, war, strife and migration.

There are many people with vested interests who would rather not collaborate with other sectors they often regard as having inimical views. Policy makers find it hard to put aside tribal interest in order to agree long-term strategies. Countries find real difficulties in working together for common goals. Much of this book sets out problems and pitfalls in identifying priorities for action and difficulties to be faced in reaching common sense solutions. Bringing the issues together in one volume will, I hope, clarify readers thoughts and stimulate helpful discussion.

**Part 1**

# The Need for Change

# Chapter 1

# Population

'Society is a contract between those who are living, those who are dead and those who are to be born'.

*Edmund Burke*

As a student studying agriculture at university in the 1960's I recall a small part of our course was devoted to what was then called 'Tropical Agriculture'. This was well before many academics began to study seriously the science and sociology of what is now widely known as 'Development Studies' – a subject which I returned to university to study after my retirement from farming in the UK in 2010. Back in the 1960's we heard stories of well-meant assistance to colonial and post-colonial countries in Africa, but which had failed disastrously. I cannot remember much about the success stories, except that they were less frequent than the failures, but I do remember one lecturer, who would nowadays be considered very politically incorrect. His summary of the problems of the 'third world', as it was then called, was that there were simply too many people, and that the cause of the recent population explosion was threefold: 'Pacification, Medication and Education'. Without these three, he said, the populations would be relatively stable as a result of continued tribal warfare and high levels of mortality through disease and malnutrition. Education, brought to them by the developed world had opened their eyes to what their lives might be, so that the 'noble savage' might aspire to be the 'consuming capitalist'. As a result, the world would soon be overburdened by an unsustainable mass of humanity.

In hindsight I realize much of this was said with a certain amount of 'tongue in cheek' but, apart from exhibiting a now outmoded view of 'colonialist' thinking, it reflected very real concerns about the significant rise in post-World war II populations in developing countries, the implications of this on finite resources, and the challenges posed for policy makers. Such concerns were not new. In 1798 an English country clergyman, by the name of Thomas Malthus, published his famous '*Essay on Population*' in which he foresaw persistent food insecurity because population numbers had begun to increase exponentially since the start of the industrial revolution in England earlier in the 18th century, whilst the ability of agriculture to produce food only increased linearly.

Fortuitously, for succeeding generations, just as Malthus forecast his domesday scenario, new lands began to be opened up for agriculture in North America and the southern hemisphere and science began to play a major role in boosting agricultural productivity. The need of plants for certain vital nutrients was recognized, and initially met using organic materials such as manure, shells and bones – later supplemented by imported sources of phosphate and nitrogen, in the form of guano (bird droppings). Supplying sufficient nitrogen to enable plant yields to be boosted much further remained a problem until the development of the Haber-Bosch process for fixing atmospheric nitrogen early in the twentieth century. Today, agriculture in the developed world relies primarily on chemical fertilisers, supplemented with sophisticated chemical compounds to control weeds and diseases. Without them the global population simply could not have grown from around one billion at the beginning of the nineteenth century to almost seven billion two centuries later.

Fast forward to 1969 when another domesday book entitled '*The Population Bomb*'[1] became an international best-seller. In it, the author, biologist Paul Ehrlich, predicted imminent and widespread famine, disease, social unrest and environmental ruin because of the same population explosion, which had caused my university lecturer to make the comments I remember all these years later. Yet again, science came to the rescue and Ehrlich's predictions did not come to pass. In the developed world plant and animal breeders enabled remarkable annual productivity gains, which only slowed at the start of the twenty first century, and perhaps only then because of reduced research investment by most governments across the world. Since 1985, however, population has grown at 2.8% annually whilst agricultural productivity growth has gone up at a rate of 1.1% [2].

The predicted mid twentieth century food catastrophe in Asia was largely averted through the work of a few scientists who produced new dwarf wheat and rice varieties that responded to increased fertilizer appli-cations without 'lodging' (that is, falling flat on the ground and being spoilt). The resultant increase in crop yields allowed the number of hungry people in the world to reduce by half, even as the global population doubled from three to six billion. The leader of this 'Green Revolution', plant breeder Norman Borlaug, earned a Nobel Prize and, to this day, his is the only statue of a non-politician in the central lobby of the US Senate.

The very success of the Green Revolution and the increasing frequency of food surpluses in developed countries from the late 1970's, which, in the EU were vilified by the media as 'grain mountains' and 'milk lakes' costing the EU taxpayers dear, led to reduced government support for agricultural research and for agriculture generally. In parallel, an increasing number of people became concerned with the damage done to the global environment by agriculture and modern agricultural practices. I will examine, in more detail later, the complex issues involved in debates between agriculturalists and environmentalists, which centre on what level and type of food production might be 'sustainable' in the twenty first century.

Until recently, population growth had slipped down the international agenda, despite increasing concerns about over-exploitation of global resources and increasing environmental damage. Some predictions suggested a levelling off of global population, by the end of the 21st century, at around 9 billion. Predictions of this kind are an inexact science, and world population could be as high as 11 billion by 2100[3], largely because African birthrates have not been declining as fast as expected. So what are the most likely outcomes for future populations? Where will growth be the greatest? What implications are there for local and global economies, for the environment, resources and also for jobs, migration patterns and, importantly for this study, for rural societies? And what might be the effect of demographic changes resulting from lower fertility rates and ageing populations, especially in the developed world?

Population studies are not simply about numbers of people. They encompass predictions about changes in age profiles within different populations, urbanization and migration between countries, contraception, general population health, mortality rates, and much more. To get a handle on the scale of changes already in train, we can expect to see, in developing countries, the equivalent of a new city of one million people built every five days from now until 2050[4]. According to the United Nations[5] the current world population of 7.6 billion is expected to reach 8.6 billion by 2030, 9.8 billion in 2050 and 11.2billion by 2100. Half of this growth is expected to be concentrated in nine countries with India, Nigeria and Pakistan filling the top three places. Africa is expected to account for more than half the total population growth between 2015 and 2050. This concentration of growth will make it more difficult to deal with poverty and inequality, combat hunger and malnutrition and provide health services and good education in these countries.

There is a close relationship between economic security, educational attainment, the outlook for child mortality and family size. Poorer families with little prospect of support to lift them out of poverty tend to want larger families. This reflects not only the increased likelihood that some of the children may die early, but also the hope that surviving children will help care for their parents in later life. Education, particularly of women, dramatically reduces the desire for more children and increases the demand for contraception. Much of this demand for modern methods of contraception is unmet and is a major cause of the persistence of high fertility in less developed countries. Some religious faiths, notably the Roman Catholic church, hold that most forms of contraception are morally unnacceptable, and do not accept the right of women to choose whether to conceive. Even more controversial in some countries is the right for women to undergo abortion.

In the last seventy years global life expectancy has increased by 50% and infant mortality has declined. Over the same period the average global citizen has become much richer. There has been an exponential rise in those who would call themselves 'middle class', fuelled particularly by the astonishing economic transformation of China, and to a lesser extent, other areas of South East Asia. One consequence of this growing and wealthier population has been a dramatic rise in both production and consumption of goods. World consumption of fossil fuels rose fourfold between 1950 and 2000 leading to soaring emissions of carbon dioxide, the major cause of climate change. Globally between 1961 and 2009 food production has increased by 115% (meat 211%)[ibid.2] and consumption in all countries except Sub Saharan Africa has increased. Most tellingly, in China between 1963 and 2003 meat consumption per capita increased by 349%, sugar by 127% and vegetable oil by 199%, and since 2003, these upward trends in consumption have continued. No wonder, then, that concern has again risen in recent years as to whether the next generation will be able to feed itself, given that there is no new land available for growing food without causing dramatic environmental destruction; the outlook for global agriculture in most climate change scenarios is for poorer yields, and more variable rainfall and greater disease pressure. I will address this in the next chapter.

All this seems distant from the experience and concerns of people living in a rich country like Britain, where, apart from worries over inward migration, there is little real understanding of the challenges posed by increasing global population. More evident, but not yet at crisis level, is the problem of an ageing population. As populations age, the proportion of working, economically-active people declines. Older people become more of a drag on the economy – their health costs are higher and are largely paid by the working population. Globally the number of people aged 60 or above is expected to more than double by 2050 and triple by 2100. In Europe one in three of the population will be over 60 years old in 2050. In Asia, Latin America and the Caribbean, where the figure is currently 12%, this will rise to 25% by 2050[ibid.5]. Only in Africa where 41% of the current population is under 15 years, will the 2050 figure for over 60's be below 10%.

Already in countries such as Japan we see significant effects of an ageing population on the economy of the country. The one-child policy in China, from 1979 means that country will move quite rapidly to a situation where the 'old' outnumber the 'young'. In parts of Europe we see a similar situation, and because they have relatively generous systems of welfare and pension provision, the expense to the public purse is becoming untenable. Increased life expectancy rates coupled with rising levels of lifestyle related chronic diseases, such as diabetes or obesity, are putting enormous strains on health budgets. I will return to these issues in later chapters too.

Those countries with more youthful populations are generally much poorer, often with only rudimentary healthcare and welfare systems. One of the biggest problems these countries will face in the coming decades is youth unemployment. Initially as a country develops mortality rates fall, but fertility and birth rates continue at a high level for some time, giving rise to a rapid spurt in population growth. Usually, this is accompanied by migration from rural areas to the cities where cheap labour fuels a rise in production, which is often exported to wealthier countries. Then comes the phase when machines replace people, particularly concentrating on the work previously done by the unskilled or less well educated. In a world where continued consumption cannot continue at an exponential rate the result is likely to be mass youth unemployment with huge implications for welfare systems, social inclusion and cultural attitudes to work. This area of concern is admirably analysed in a report by The Oxford Martin Commission for Future Generations (Oct. 2013) entitled 'Now for the Long Term[6].

If problems such as education, infrastructure development and corruption can be addressed in the younger nations, their potential for economic growth is greater than those countries whose economies are increasingly weighed down by an ageing population. However, there is a general trend for the young to migrate to cities, leaving the older generations in rural areas. This may not be all bad because although labour might be lost from rural areas, increased earnings and remittances home from the younger generation may allow for compensating investments and then hiring of additional labour on farm[7]. Ultimately, however, as can be starkly seen in most developed economies such as the UK, too few young people come to regard agriculture as a rewarding career.

The industrial revolution in Britain during the eighteenth and nineteenth centuries dramatically changed the face of the country from a largely rural society to an urban one. A similar rural exodus is taking place now in developing nations. In 2010, for the first time in human history, the global population living in cities exceeded the number living in rural areas. By 2015 the proportion in cities was up to 55%. This has a number of important implications for demand for food and for the type of food required. Most (75%)[ibid.2] of the global poor live in rural areas. Many of these are smallholder farmers. Although living conditions in urban slums give the impression that the poor are generally urban dwellers, the statistics show that urban incomes are higher. In consequence, there are differences in total expenditure on food, and in the type of food demanded, as illustrated by figures given earlier on changes in Chinese consumption patterns as the country urbanized.

Adding together the likely global changes in consumption of food as populations increase in size and wealth, it is clear that the food system will need to meet significantly greater demands placed on it over the coming decades. Estimates vary between 50% and 70% more food being needed by 2050, depending on rate of economic progress, dietary trends and whether we can reduce food wastage and improve efficiency of production and utilization. These and other issues will determine the pressure on available agricultural land, on water supplies, plant nutrients and food supplies for animals producing meat and milk.

Before we examine, in detail, the possible pathways for future food systems it is appropriate to remind ourselves of the interconnectedness of the modern world. This book deliberately sets out to present problems in a global context, because so many of them do not respect country boundaries. Population pressures, continuing inequalities of opportunity, shortages of natural resources, hunger, poverty, unemployment and war are all causes of migration of people from poorer countries to richer ones. Although most migration is within countries, from rural areas to towns and cities, cross-border migration is an increasing issue for politicians in the developed world. This problem looks set to grow in coming years.

In 2016 the World Economic Forum published its *Global Risk Report 2016*[8] , prioritizing the impact and likelihood of risks to world order over the following decade. Top of the list of 'likely' risks was 'large scale involuntary migration' (largely reflecting severe unrest in the Arab and Muslim world). This also came fourth on the list for 'impact'. Severe risks to world order as a whole appear to be increasing, and these risks are closely interlinked. In terms of 'likelihood', 'extreme weather events' came second to migration, followed by 'failure of climate change mitigation and adaptation'. This last risk came top of the list for the greatest potential impact. So it is to climate change and in particular its likely impact on food security and food systems that I now turn.

# Chapter 2

# Climate Change

'Things that can't go on forever, don't'.

*Herb Stein (economist)*

I find it hard to credit, but there are still a lot of 'dinosaurs' out there who maintain that global warming is a conspiracy dreamed up by scientists with their own agenda to change the world order. Despite the science pointing ever more surely at human induced change in the climate, a few hardy sceptics still maintain their total rejection of the evidence. Climate forecasts are naturally plagued with variability of outcome, and the sceptics use the lack of certainty in predictions of future climatic changes to deny that anything is amiss with the world.

More dangerous to future generations than these few fanatics is a large number of individuals and companies who recognize that climate change is real, but, for a variety of reasons choose to believe that it is not of immediate importance to do much about it. A study carried out by Non Governmental Organisations before the United Nations COP21 climate conference in December 2014[1] found that nearly half of the world's biggest companies actively fight regulation to protect the climate. Energy companies score very poorly, and oil companies worst of all, as might be expected, given that their business models are threatened. Chemical companies follow closely behind, but the worst offender in this survey was Koch industries, an American firm with energy and agricultural interests, which has a long track record of financing climate-sceptic research, and supporting politicians to fight environmental regulation in the US. Unsurprisingly the Koch organisation was a major funder of the campaign by Donald Trump to be US President in 2017.

Mainly right-leaning politicians in many countries are openly hostile to the science behind global warming, partly on the basis, it would appear, that action to mitigate the potential effects would increase the role of

Government and reduce the freedom of the market economy to make its own choices. In a world where it is increasingly evident that resources are limited and that we have already crossed a number of 'planetary boundaries' (see note below), it is clear that market based capitalism needs to rethink fundamentally how to proceed. Sadly, few economists seem prepared to offer effective arguments for necessary change. In addition, the short-term nature of political decision-making tends to push the longer term threats down the priority list, particularly when they are so seemingly unpalatable as climate change, and require concerted action from other countries which are all seeking advantage for themselves.

---

**Planetary Boundaries**[2]: A concept of 9 earth system processes which had boundaries proposed in 2009 by a group of earth system and environmental scientists led by Johan Rockstrom from the Stockholm Resilience Centre and Will Steffen from the Australian National University. The group wanted to define a 'safe operating space for humanity'. They assert that once human activity has passed certain thresholds or tipping points, defined as 'planetary boundaries', there is a risk of 'irreversible and abrupt environmental change'.

---

The main problem in dealing with climate change is not scientific uncertainty, but the inability of political systems to respond prudently to scientific risk when there is little political reward. Taking action to reduce greenhouse gas emissions is politically thankless, despite the fact that not taking action may have terrible results a few years down the line. Resources expended today will only show results well into the future. Yet because carbon dioxide ($CO_2$) remains in the atmosphere for more than 100 years what is emitted today leads to changes which are essentially irrevocable in terms of human life span. There are other greenhouse gases with particular relevance to agriculture, such as methane ($CH_4$) and nitrous oxide ($N_2O$), which we will examine later, and these have shorter life-spans in the atmosphere than $CO_2$, but are still very important in the overall heating force on the atmosphere.

In capitalist democracies companies and politicians can be persuaded to change through shareholder activism and public pressure. Whilst there are areas where such action is changing attitudes, it is, so far, very limited in scope. A number of international companies have incorporated declarations of intent in their Corporate Social Responsibility Statements whilst cities such as New York and Bogota have set their own emission standards in advance of any national measures. But UK consumer research in 2007 and repeated in 2013[3] pointed to public attitudes trending in the wrong direction. In 2007 32% felt they could influence policy on global warming but by 2013 this had reduced to 21%. In America a survey by Pew Research and Gallup found that 83% of Americans acknowledged that global warming would be problem in the future, but those same people ranked the issue near the bottom of their priority list, well behind jobs, the economy and health care[4].

In May 2019 the UK Committee on Climate Change[5] published its report on how the UK should address the issue. It set out in some detail the actions required in each major sector of the economy, including agriculture. It made the case for the UK to lead the world to a greener future. The truth is neither individuals nor individual countries will succeed in solving the problem of climate change. It is a problem to be addressed by the world acting in concert. Lord Nicholas Stern, author of the seminal work on the economics of climate change *The Economics of Climate Change*[6,] believes there are two defining challenges, namely '*Managing climate change and overcoming poverty*'. He believes if we fail to manage climate change we will create an environment so hostile that lives and livelihoods will be destroyed. But if we try to manage climate change in ways which put obstacles in the way of overcoming poverty, we will not have the coalition we need to manage climate change. Poorer nations and peoples will not, and cannot suffer the worst effects of climate change caused to a great extent by wealthier nations. This raises the stakes and the complexity of the problem very significantly. And it makes the problems and the solutions more difficult for the general public to understand, and to believe that their actions will make a difference.

Sadly the level of understanding of the science of climate change among both the general public, (and many politicians – who, nevertheless are often keen to pontificate on the subject), is poor. At the same time, when the first damaging effects of climate change are even now being felt largely in poorer and developing countries, the empathy felt by many in the developed world toward their plight is lessening. Migration flows are increasing nationalistic tendencies and populist reaction against globalisation is making nations more inward looking and less inclined to work for the common good. So, although it is not the prime purpose of this book to make the case for action to mitigate climate change, it is important to set out, in very basic terms why so many scientists are worried.

The world is getting warmer. In the last 100 years the average temperature of the Earth's surface has increased by 1°C. Seventeen of the eighteen warmest years on record were in the first eighteen years of the 21st century. The atmosphere of the earth traps some of the suns energy naturally in the atmosphere, but human activities such as burning fossil fuels, cutting down forests, increasing cultivation of land and fertiliser use adds to the natural greenhouse effect primarily by adding more carbon dioxide, which is able to absorb more of the suns energy than the other gases. For the first time in 800,000 years the concentration of $CO_2$ in the atmosphere rose above 400 parts per million in 2015. If no action were taken this could rise to 750ppm within a century, implying a likely average global temperature increase of between 4° and 6°C. Such temperatures have not been seen on earth for tens of millions of years, and never experienced by humans (who only came on the scene some 250,000 years ago).

The really important point to recognize is that the less we do now, the more we will have to do later, and at considerably higher cost. This point is disputed by Lord Lawson in his book *An Appeal to Reason – a cool look at global warming*[7]. His argument is that it is best to wait and react to problems when they arise. I believe this to be not only economically wrong but morally perverse. Our generation largely caused the problem. We should not leave it to our children to clear up the mess – assuming they can, which is unlikely, since changes will be irreversible within any human lifespan. There is an increasing risk as time goes by that we will not be able to hold the rise in temperature below what was until recently regarded as a (fairly) safe level of 2°C. Following the Paris agreement in 2015 scientists were commissioned to examine the probable differences between an average 1.5° rise and 2°. Their report to the 2018 Katowice conference showed beyond doubt that the extra 0.5° will cause very significant additional problems for biodiversity and for human wellbeing in many countries. Even at 1.5°C it is extremely likely there will be severe consequences, including significant sea level rise, biodiversity loss, increasingly severe weather events and large areas of the world suffering worse water shortages. Beyond 2°C would be to enter unknown territory, with the potential for the climate to pass one or more 'tipping points', where dramatic changes take place. One of these may be the failure of the Gulf

Stream, which currently keeps Britain and Western Europe much warmer than their latitude would suggest. Paradoxically, therefore, excess global warming could mean Britain becomes considerably colder, while other parts of the world become unbearably hot.

To give an idea of timescales, the next few years, up to 2030 are critical to achieving both the 1.5° and 2° trajectories. The Paris Agreement (2015) ended with 195 nations agreeing to restrict global emissions of greenhouse gases (GHG's) to achieve, if possible, a global temperature rise over pre-industrial levels of 1.5°C, and well below the 'risky' 2° level. But the agreement is not legally binding and some countries are more important than others in reaching the global target. Although in 1992, when climate talks first began, 2/3rds of GHG emissions came from developed countries, by 2015, 2/3rds came from the developing world. China is now the largest emitter at 24%[8] followed by the USA at 12%, EU at 9%, India at 6%, Brazil 6%, Russia 5% and Japan 3%. For the first time at Copenhagen there was agreement by both China and USA to join in the deal – vital if any serious progress is to be made. By 2017, with President Trump in the White House, the US commitment to the Paris accord was withdrawn.

The inevitable tendency of politicians to place unpalatable decisions in 'the too difficult box' is profoundly misguided. We have already established that greenhouse gases are not transitory, but remain in the atmosphere for a very long time with incremental consequences. Meanwhile economies continue to develop and invest in the future. A great deal of infrastructure and capital investment, particularly in energy and transport, is long term. This results in 'technological lock-in' where, for instance, we see continued investment in coal-fired power stations in India with an investment life stretching forward many decades. This is despite India's own finance ministry publishing an economic survey suggesting climate change could shrink agricultural income in India by up to 25% on unirrigated land, and 18% in irrigated areas by 2100[9]. Fossil fuel companies and their institutional investors (which often include Governments) seem to be banking on failure to agree controls on climate change. Despite the world having five times more coal, oil and gas on current inventories than many scientists believe it is safe to burn[10] they are still scouring the world for more reserves, which ought to be left in the ground. By mid 2018 American fracking output from shale oil deposits raised the US to first place in world oil production. Yet for countries whose economies currently benefit hugely from fossil fuels there are real danger signals ahead. As Sheikh Yamani, erstwhile secretary of OPEC famously observed, '*The stone age did not end because we ran out of stones, and it will be the same with fossil fuels*'.

Delay in changing to investments, which are designed to meet future needs within acceptable climatic boundaries, increases both risk and cost if locked-in capital has to be written off. Developing economies which, today emit a very small proportion of global GHG's, (yet stand to suffer the worst effects of climatic change – see later), need support to develop their economies on the right trajectory if they are not to add to global problems in future. Many of the disagreements in climate talks have centred on the issue of who pays to put matters right, and on the rights of less developed countries to grow their economies (and their GHG emissions) to pull their people out of poverty.

After a quarter of a century of work by scientists across the globe there is a vast body of data supporting the need for action. It is clear from this data that the risks and likely outcomes resulting from global warming are very different from place to place. In Africa key risks identified[11] include extreme drought and stress on water resources, reduced crop productivity associated with heat and drought stress, and likely increase in the geographical range of vector and water-borne diseases. In Europe, key risks are increased economic losses from increasing sea level and river flooding, increased water restrictions, especially in southern Europe, and increased heat related events causing economic loss, incidence of wildfires and poorer air quality. In Asia there is likely to be increased river, coastal and urban flooding, increased heat-related mortality and increased drought-related water and food shortage causing malnutrition.

Paradoxically, it is at the coldest points on earth where global warming will have its largest effect. At the poles ice is melting at an alarming rate. The extent of both arctic and antarctic sea ice show consistently downward trends since 1980. This has implications for global sea levels with recent predictions pointing to an increasing rate of annual sea level rise from around 3mm per annum now to 1cm per annum by 2100[12].

Clearly these summaries give only a flavor of what different populations might expect, and within each region risks and responses to them will vary dramatically. Although climatic change is a global phenomenon the responses to it must be local. There is no one size fits all solution, and each society needs to work out its own way of dealing with the problems. Already we begin to see how our global decision makers must juggle with many problem 'balls in the air' at the same time. 'Joining up the dots' both globally and locally will not be easy!

So far we have talked about the need to 'mitigate' climate change, to reduce its potential effects by taking pre-emptive action. In this sense, mitigation policies can be thought of as 'climate insurance'. But already many societies are feeling the consequences of a climate which is already changing, from loss of arctic sea ice to increased severity of storm events in the tropics. This requires societies to adapt to new conditions, and 'adaptation' is the fall-back position of some climate change deniers who argue that adapting to meet known problems is more sensible than pre-emptive action against unknown ones. As I have demonstrated, this is a view, which disregards the scientific evidence and leads, at the least, to much higher costs in future years, and at worst, disastrous and irreversible climate change.

Such short sighted views also pay little heed to the time lag for new research and innovatory techniques to develop and become common practice. In the Foreword I cited the example from plant breeding, where the need for development of varieties capable of growing in significantly different conditions is widely accepted. To see those varieties taken up into widespread practice, can take more than 20 years, even in a well ordered society where new technology is rapidly disseminated. In low income countries where both the science and the infrastructure is lacking, the time required may be even longer. As I shall discuss later, changing eating habits or lifestyles such as introducing new technologies such as electric cars may take longer still. Waiting to see what might happen is not a sensible option. The next chapter looks more closely at the interplay between climate change and agriculture.

# Chapter 3

# Climate change and Agriculture

'Only a crisis, actual or perceived, produces real change'.

*Milton Friedman (economist)*

The agricultural sector will be hit hard by climate change. Work done for the British Department for International Development (DfID) by the CGIAR Research Programme on Climate Change, Agriculture and Food Security[1] estimates that over the next 40 years more than 265 million people face a 5% decrease in growing season duration due to an increasingly variable and hotter climate sweeping the globe. Detailed work by the same programme[2] analysed the effects of climate change on 22 important agricultural commodities in the developing world. It concluded that climate change introduced a significant hurdle to the world food system being able to feed a projected population of around 10 billion in 2050. More particularly, the provision of adequate calories and protein for many poorer populations would be a real problem because yields and viability of the most common staple crops – wheat, maize and rice – will be challenged by new weather patterns and in some areas livestock and aquatic production could also be hit. High $CO_2$ levels also increase the risk of poorer populations, who rely on plant based protein for their diet, (76% world population), running into protein, iron and zinc deficiency, since levels of these nutrients appear to be adversely affected by $CO_2$ concentration[3].

Whole regions face a shift to a different type of climate, with consequent effects on the crops that can be grown. Some regions already experience the consequences of a 1.5°C rise despite the global average being 1°C currently. As a result, many people face the likelihood of having to adapt to different food systems from the ones to which they are traditionally accustomed. Farmers certainly need to react to changing climate by developing new techniques to grow existing crops or livestock, or in some cases embracing entirely new enterprises. If this transition is to be successful, a great deal more targeted research, on a region by region basis will need to be carried out, together with adequate education and extension services to enable new ideas to translate into practical production.

It seems likely that warmer temperatures will increase the range and prevalence of many pests and diseases. Increased frequency of drought could put the future of grazing livestock at risk in more marginal areas such as the savannah lands south of the Sahara desert in Africa. As with crops, there is an increased likelihood of wider incidence of animal diseases. Soya bean is a major source of vegetable protein for humans and animals. It is, however, very susceptible to increased temperatures and although new lands may become suitable for the crop at higher latitudes, this may not compensate for reductions in the main exporting regions of the US and Brazil.

As always with complex predictions about biological systems there is a degree of uncertainty of outcomes, which encourages those critics who argue for certainty before committing investment. American researchers[4] at Stanford University produced an assessment on the effects of climate change on global yields of wheat and maize over the period 2014 – 2024, and calculated the chances of current level of crop yield improvement reducing by half. They found a 1 in 4 chance of this happening for maize, and a 1 in 6 chance for wheat. To some that may be an argument for doing nothing now, but if taken within the context that existing rates of technological advance are already insufficient to meet likely future demand, and that pressure to reduce the environmental impact of agricultural practices will increasingly bear down on yields, then doing nothing sounds a very risky option indeed.

It cannot be stressed enough that some areas of the world are much more vulnerable to climate induced food insecurity than others. Sadly, most of these are in poorer countries, where a combination of factors increases the vulnerability of their populations. Global risks analytics company, Maplecroft[5], produce an annual Climate Change and Environmental Risk Atlas which identifies 32 extreme risk countries, based on the ability of the people to cope with problems, the physical exposure of countries to climatic change and on government capacity to adapt to that change over the next 30 years. A unifying characteristic of these vulnerable economies is their heavy reliance on agriculture, with 65% of the population employed in the sector and 28% of their overall economic output coming from agricultural revenues. Most of these countries are in sub-saharan Africa or in South East Asia. According to the UN, IPPC figures estimate declines of up to 50% in staple food production such as rice, wheat and maize in some locations over the next 35 years.

Food insecurity and food price volatility are often the result of variability of weather systems. On a global scale such variation accounts for a third of crop yield variability[6]. This translates into large annual fluctuations in global crop production, which, in turn leads to price 'spikes' and regional shortages. Nobel prizewinner and economist Amartya Sen commented, *'Starvation is the characteristic of* <u>*some people*</u> *not having enough food to eat. It is not the characteristic of there not being* <u>*enough*</u> *to eat'* (my underlining). Prolonged drought, flooding or excessive heat, are major causes of social unrest. Lack of bread and lack of hope are triggers for many of the conflicts we see in the world today. Climate change has the potential to exacerbate conflict and make it more difficult to improve food security and help reduce tensions. In the chapter on population I referred to the inevitability of increased migration from vulnerable and unstable countries. Adverse climate change adds another reason to believe this will be so.

Clearly, in a warming world there will be 'winners' as well as losers, at least in the short and medium term. Global climate models have been used to predict how changing climates might affect the suitability of land for various types of agriculture[7]. Northern latitudes, especially in Canada, China and Russia should gain an additional 5.6m square kilometres of cropland, whilst mainly tropical lands in the global south and the Mediterranean will decline in suitability. In these areas too, the amount of land suitable for multiple annual cropping also decreases, especially in sub-saharan Africa and Brazil. Such calculations do not take into account the fact that many of the newly suitable areas are sparsely populated and lack both labour and infrastructure. But neither do they consider adaptive measures such as improved irrigation in some of the climate affected areas. What is clear, however, is that vulnerable countries risk becoming even more vulnerable without assistance from wealthier nations, and that, morality apart, there is a case to be made for such help being in the interests of the donor nations, by reducing migration pressure and the likelihood of conflict.

Of course the food system, including agriculture, is not simply a passive casualty of climate change. It is both one of the major contributors to GHG emissions and also has the potential to be part of the solution to capturing some of the excess $CO_2$ that is at the root of the problem. When the entire food system is taken into account estimates by the United Nations[8] put greenhouse gas emissions from the sector between 43%-57% of the total. Agricultural production accounts for between 11-15%, processing, transport, packaging and retail, a further 15-20%, and waste between 2-4%. The balance 15-18% is an estimate of land use change globally, including deforestation, the majority of which is closely related to the demand for food and is a major player in the destruction of the natural environment.

A more widely accepted figure of 25% of GHG emissions does not include waste or land use change, but even this is a substantial proportion of total global emissions. Yet agriculture, until 2018, barely figured in the UN climate talks, neither acknowledging the significant impact of the sector, nor the positive role it could play in mitigating the effects. At the UN talks in Paris in 2015 there was agreement to try to keep below 2°C rise in global average temperature, but to aim for 1.5°C if possible, as a safer option. According to Prof. Tim Benton, (UK Government Czar on food security), the emissions pathway the world would need to follow for a 66% chance of staying within 1.5°C would require every other human activity, except the food sector to be stop all its carbon emissions by 2050. He concludes that our demand for food alone virtually guarantees the Paris aspirations unachievable without significant changes to the food system[9].

Globally soils contain more than double the amount of carbon in the atmosphere and three times the amount stored in plants, animals and micro-organisms. Where environments are undisturbed, such as native forest or rangeland the gains and losses of soil carbon are roughly balanced. Plants take up $CO_2$ from the atmosphere and convert it through photosynthesis to organic matter. When the plant decays part of the trapped carbon and other nutrients remain in the soil as humus. But when the land is disturbed by cultivation, or plant and animal remains are not recycled but consumed elsewhere, the balance is disturbed. Over centuries farmers have mined soils to grow food, releasing, in the process, some of the stored carbon as $CO_2$.

The challenge is to put some of this back into the soil through the process of carbon sequestration. Improving soils by increasing depleted organic matter is in the long term interests of farmers, since organic matter is crucial to soil structure, moisture holding capacity and 'workability', as well as providing a nutrient 'buffer' thereby reducing the risk of soil supply not meeting crop demand. But short term interests in gaining a financial return, having little security of land tenure, or having no other means of survival but to 'mine' the soil often prevail. In the UK it can be shown that when crop values are low, key nutrient applications are reduced. Pressures to specialize in order to maintain profitability lead, in cropping areas, to reduction in organic manures derived from animal wastes. In consequence the average UK arable soil organic matter is between 3% and 3.5%, with many soils below the 3% level. A target of 5% would be optimal.

Methane ($CH_4$) is another greenhouse gas, which is more powerful than $CO_2$ at retaining heat in the atmosphere, but remains there for less time. Grazing ruminant livestock are a major source of $CH_4$ and the UK Committee on Climate Change report (2019)[10] proposes a reduction in grazing livestock in order to reduce emissions. In parallel it suggests very significant increase in tree planting, to absorb atmospheric $CO_2$ in wood biomass and restoration of peatland to sequester carbon in soil organic matter. For farmers to make any of these changes will require significant and long term government incentives.

Many soils in Africa are easily degraded when continuously cultivated. In almost every measure of degradation the trajectory is downwards as a result of population pressure, inadequate environmental management and lack of nutrient replenishment[11]. Yields are low and the widespread use of modern technology is vital both to improve soil management and increase productivity to feed burgeoning populations. Yet, as we shall see later, intensification of production involving additional inputs such as inorganic fertilisers brings its own problems.

While cost effective technologies for soil carbon sequestration are still to be developed, there are a number of pilot projects being trialled in different regions of the world. Most are based on local forms of direct sowing of crops or minimal tillage systems to reduce soil disturbance. These are often combined with diverse crop rotations, designed to replace some of the lost nutrients, and cover cropping to minimize the amount of bare soil subject to damage from erosion and leaching of nutrients through the soil profile. Particularly in tropical areas there is merit in reviewing traditional approaches by techniques such as inter-cropping with legumes, which 'fix' nitrogen in the soil, mixing crops with livestock and trees, conserving water by building bunds or pits, and erecting or growing windbreaks to minimize wind erosion.

There are very strong environmental grounds for limiting the expansion of agricultural land at the expense of rainforest or natural grasslands. Not only does disturbance of 'virgin' land release a significant pulse of carbon to the atmosphere, but the loss of biodiversity is very serious. The rainforest is the most ecologically diverse environment on earth. Yet this environment has been plundered in recent decades for (often) illegal logging, conversion to grazing land and to palm oil plantations. Deforestation and forest degradation still account for 10-11% of global greenhouse gas emissions[12]. Agriculture is Africa's largest economic sector and more than 25% of the world's arable land lies in the continent (including 60% of the world total of uncultivated arable land[13]). But this generates only 10% of global agricultural output, so there is huge potential here for increasing yields as well as expanding cultivated acres, but as already noted, the management of the delicate African soils needs significant improvement, involving education, infrastructure, good governance, clarity of land tenure and adequate finance. And increasing cultivated land area threatens biodiversity and exacerbates climatic change.

If we are serious in our resolve to tackle climate change, it is, therefore, inevitable that agriculture and food will need to play a very significant role. What form should this role take? Is it possible for the food system to reduce substantially its own contribution to climate change whilst increasing production to meet increased demand, and reducing environmental impact and sequestering large amounts of carbon? Is it possible to make sense of so much complexity? And there are still a large number of interacting issues I have not yet discussed, which interact with climate change and the food system, compounding the web of challenges facing policy makers. The first of these is water.

# Chapter 4

# Water

'I am I plus my surroundings, and if I do not preserve the latter I do not preserve myself'.

*Jose Ortega Gasset (Spanish philosopher)*

It's not that the earth is short of water. Salt water covers two thirds of the planet and if all the fresh water resources, including those trapped in snow and ice, were evenly spread, I would not be highlighting it as a challenge. But, as we know, it is expensive in terms of energy use and money to desalinate seawater, and while some areas of the world receive too much rain, others receive too little. What is more, rain often falls at times and in quantities not ideal for plant growth. Much of the excess rain runs back to the sea, although some is trapped in underground aquifers, lakes or glaciers. Sadly, an increasing proportion of this water picks up pollutants, largely as a result of man's activities, and the ecological cost of this is seen in river deltas and in streams and lakes devoid of wildlife, and in groundwater no longer fit to drink. Waste products from industry and from consumers are well regulated in some countries but not in others. Some attract more publicity than others, such as waste plastic – brought to the world's attention largely through a popular wildlife programme on TV. Agriculture contributes significantly to water pollution, most critically through the loss of nitrate and phosphate leached from soils before being used by growing crops. The resultant eutrophication (depletion of oxygen via stimulation of algal growth) in water severely affects fish and other aquatic life and according to Rockstrom[1] the world has already exceeded its planetary boundary for nitrate beyond which there is a risk of abrupt and irreversible environmental change.

Scientists estimate that around 70% of the impact of climate change affects the water sector, and that 90% of natural disasters are linked to it. *'In almost every region of the world, population growth, rapid urbanization, rising levels of consumption, desertification, land degradation and climate change have combined to leave countries suffering from severe water scarcity[2].'* Almost everywhere the incidence of flooding caused by more intense rainfall has increased. Severe rainfall events cause erosion and crop loss in agriculture, increasing financial risk and price volatility. This is a topic to which I will return in a later chapter, because it affects investment and makes farmers in all countries more risk-averse.

In South America the Andean glaciers, which provide vital water resources to millions of people, are shrinking. In the Asia-Pacific region the number of record breaking rainfall events increased by 56% over the 1981-2010 period[2ibid] making this the world's most disaster prone region. Many of the biggest cities in the world are at risk of severe flooding within the next 50 years as sea levels rise.

The Asian region also suffers from poor hygiene standards and as much as 30% of the population uses drinking water contaminated by human faeces. The critical role of water, sanitation and hygiene is widely recognized, yet diarrhoeal disease is the second leading cause of death in children under five[3] and significantly increases the risk of stunting. And there are many other water-borne diseases, including malaria and Zika virus, which appear to be spreading more widely with climate change.

The rapid development of China since the 1980's has been accompanied by over-exploitation of water resources, unchecked pollution and increasing problems of drought. Increasing water demand and over-exploitation of groundwater reserves affect not only China, but vast areas of West Asia, the Middle East and western USA. Although Africa as a whole has ample freshwater, there are significant areas where water scarcity reduces agricultural productivity and food security. Inefficient irrigation practices, over cultivation and over grazing together with climate change, results in considerable soil degradation and loss every year.

Perhaps the most profound changes to the global water system is happening, as a result of ongoing climate change in the Arctic. Warming here has increased at twice the global average since 1980 with a progressive decrease in the extent of summer sea ice. The effect on threatened species such as the polar bear is well known. Less well known is the implication for sea level rise as vast quantities of melting ice from glaciers across the globe add to the volume of the oceans. The volume of freshwater from the Greenland glaciers could well trigger a slowing or cessation of the Gulf Stream current, which keeps Western Europe warmer than its latitude would suggest. And even though 1°C does not sound much, any warming of the oceans leads to an expansion in volume, and hence to a sea level rise globally. Low lying Pacific islands are already threatened with inundation and whole countries, such as Bangladesh and the Maldives are at risk within a few decades, unless global action is taken urgently.

Yet water scarcity in other parts of the world is perhaps a bigger challenge still. Just south of the Sahara desert, Lake Chad was the 6th largest freshwater lake in the world 50 years ago, but has now shrunk to less than half its previous size. As the water disappeared so too did the livelihoods of many living around its shores. In places this has led to violent conflict. More than 1 billion people currently live in water scarce regions, and as many as 3.5 billion, (almost half the total world population), could experience water scarcity by 2050[4]. If the world carries on using water in the same inefficient ways that it does now, the World Bank[5] estimates that severe water scarcity will affect much of Africa, the Middle East, central and southern Asia, including Pakistan, India and China – all of those areas, in fact, where dramatic population growth and increased demand for water is expected. Even with more efficient allocation and use of water, many of these regions will still face considerable problems. The worst affected regions could see their economic growth decline by as much as 6% due to water related impacts on agriculture, health and incomes [ibid].

As a result both governments and industry are looking for ways to better manage consumption, often through public policy change that restricts usage, as well as investing in new technologies and innovation. But economic growth is a thirsty business. By 2050, global water demand is projected to increase by 55%[6] mainly due to growing demands from manufacturing, thermal electricity generation and domestic use. This poses particular problems to the food sector because agriculture and food currently accounts for 70% of global freshwater consumption. At the same time, some estimates suggest it will need to produce 60% more food globally, and perhaps the bigger proportion of this in developing countries where population and consumption pressures are highest.

Something has to give! The growth rate of global agricultural water demand is not sustainable. Efficiency of of water use within the sector needs to increase substantially. In many areas there are obvious ways to improve efficiency through better irrigation technology, or through construction of water storage reservoirs to store excess and off-season rainfall. But technologies such as drip irrigation are expensive, and often beyond the means of smaller farmers, especially those in poorer countries. In some areas education in better water management, such as mulching and small-scale collection of rainwater in cisterns will help, but in others it may be necessary to reduce dependence on irrigation, or even to stop food production altogether. In California, for instance, following a prolonged period of drought and over exploitation of groundwater reserves, some farmers switched from high water demanding crops such as alfalfa, almonds and rice, to less water intensive grains and vegetables. By contrast, in parts of Latin America and Sub-Saharan Africa, where there are adequate, untapped water supplies, new irrigation schemes will probably be developed as local and international demand for food increases.

Governments have a role in developing ways to manage consumption better through policy and regulatory changes. Water pricing is widely suggested as a method of directing scarce water supplies to the most economically beneficial use. With both regulation and pricing there needs to be adequate safeguarding to ensure adequate supplies to poor households, the environment, and to farmers who might, on simple monetary analysis be toward the bottom of the affordability league in purchasing water. Even this presumes that all parties will abide by the rules. The 2016 Global Water Integrity Outlook[7] suggests that corruption is responsible for $75 billion in losses for the water sector worldwide. Although China is notably reticent in admitting governmental failings, it is interesting that in May 2016 the National Peoples Conference[8] announced the beginning of a nationwide inspection of water conservation law enforcement to aid water conservation and strengthen protection of water resources.

A number of innovative approaches to more efficient water use in agriculture are already available, such as Climate Smart Agriculture (CSA) or Sustainable Agricultural Intensification (SAI), which allow farms to maintain, or even increase yields, whilst reducing their energy and water footprint[5ibid]. Current uptake of these techniques is slow, partly because of insufficient incentives or assistance to invest, and partly because of insufficient advisory or educational input. The potential for yield increases through improved crop water management is particularly large in water scarce regions such as China, Australia, western USA, Mexico and South Africa according to a 2016 computer simulation study[9].

Agriculture comprises 3.7% of South African GDP and employs 13.5% of the labour force. The country is 90% self sufficient for food, most of which comes from rain-fed land. Of the 10% of land that is irrigated more than half is watered through relatively efficient sprinkler or drip irrigation systems[10]. However, demand for food and animal feed is rising, climate is becoming more unpredictable and demands for water for domestic and industrial use is increasing particularly in the fast expanding urban areas. Available water supplies in 2017/18 in many parts of the country reached record lows. Here in microcosm are the challenges facing many other areas of the world. Solutions will involve tough trade-offs between the competing demands of agriculture, industry and a large and growing urban sector.

Even within one region, such as South Africa, there is no one size-fits-all solution. Local areas need local solutions to take into account a different balance of social, environmental and economic need. This is equally true in well-developed economies, such as my own region of East Anglia, where the local water agency is developing 'catchment area' plans in cooperation with stakeholders representing the diverse interests of people and businesses in these local areas. The aim is to produce integrated management plans through discussion and agreement, thereby improving understanding of the wider 'water economy' and avoiding, so far as possible, future conflict between competing interests.

Where water crises are already evident this kind of agreed solution may prove very difficult to achieve. In the Middle East and South East Asia, violent conflict over water rights is already occurring, especially where there are also existing national or tribal rivalries. Many commentators believe that conflicts over water availability will fuel future wars. In such circumstances, environmental considerations are often pushed well into the background. I will be looking in more depth at the environment versus agriculture debate, but it is important to note the importance of water, both for the health and the maintenance of the natural environment on which we all ultimately rely for our survival.

In this context I want to introduce the relatively new concept of 'ecosystem services', in which water plays a major role. This recognizes the complex interaction of environmental factors which provide us with many of the necessary things to sustain life and to make it pleasurable, but to which we ascribe little or no monetary value. Clean water, clean air, the aesthetic value of nature and biodiversity, the natural systems which keep the atmosphere in balance and maintain the health of the oceans and the land. Together these constitute 'services' which we cannot do without, yet they are largely taken for granted in an economic system which only values things with price tags attached.

It is immediately evident why scientists are keen for this concept to be more widely understood. In the brave new world of post Brexit Britain most farm payments from Government are likely to be in return for environmental goods (including ecosystem services) provided by farmers. Greenhouse gas emissions continue to fuel climate change because we have so far failed to build in sufficient disincentives for people to pollute the atmosphere or to stop damaging the huge carbon 'sinks' represented by peatlands, particularly in South East Asia where palm oil plantations have replaced much of the original forested wetlands. If we use all our freshwater for agriculture, industry or domestic consumption, or if we pollute it with fertilisers, industrial chemicals or sewage to the point where it damages the wider environment, then the ability of that wider environment to provide us with 'services' diminishes. We damage our longer-term prospects in the search for short-term gain.

So there is good reason for agricultural systems to be managed in such a way that they not only produce food, but also deliver a whole range of other ecosystem services necessary for long-term food security. Many would argue that modern intensive agricultural systems fail to do this, and I will discuss this in more detail later in the book. For now, I merely note that water resources need to be shared not simply between competing economic interests, including agriculture, but also with those non-economic, and largely environmental interests vital to sustainability. As examples we should aim to keep a minimum level of river flow consistent with maintaining ecological balance, and maintain sufficient tree cover in upland areas to trap excess water flows which might cause flooding downstream. Though there are huge regional variations, one modelling study[11] concluded that meeting this minimum flow parameter is perhaps the single greatest challenge to agricultural water supply.

Such laudable aims are often difficult to achieve when human pressures on water supplies are very high. As barriers to international trade have reduced in recent years there has been a corresponding increase in agricultural trade using comparative productivity advantages between countries. The UK, in 2016, imported over 50% of its food and animal feed, partly because the products cannot be grown in the UK, but partly because some products are produced more cheaply abroad. This may be due to better climate, cheaper labour cost, or less regulation. Perversely, because water is under valued even in areas of scarcity, a significant amount of UK food comes from such areas, exacerbating their water problems. The term 'virtual water' has been coined to describe this unseen 'export' of water. In parallel, the idea of 'water footprint' is gaining credibility, to describe the 'hungriness' for water of particular crop or animal systems or particular dietary choices. For the average UK diet the most water hungry ingredients are dairy, rice, citrus fruit, pigmeat and sugar, and two thirds of that is associated with food imports produced with water which did not fall on UK soil[12]. On a world scale the 2011 UK Foresight Report[13] estimated that exported foods made up 16% to 26% of the total water used for food production, suggesting *significant potential for more efficient global use of water via trade*.

So as with climate change, solutions to global water challenges cannot be dealt with by individual countries in isolation. They form a significant part of the climate challenge; in places there is too much water at the 'wrong' time, while in other places there is too little; increasing demands pose difficulties with allocation of available water resources; there are technological and sociological issues to overcome; environmental aspects have to be given more prominence in future plans, and it may be appropriate to review our dietary habits to take more account of what effect our 'virtual water' consumption has on regions and populations beyond our shores. The benefits of co-ordinating policy for water, nutrition and health are evident, but particularly in developing countries, where such policies are not widely carried out[3ibid].

Water is one major component of productive capacity. Another is soil, and it is to consideration of the world's soils that I turn next.

# Chapter 5

# Soil

'The nation that destroys its soil destroys itself.'

*Franklin D Roosevelt*

I bought my farm in the early 1970's for just under £300 per acre. At the time this was considered expensive, but the chance to buy within a given area often only comes once in a generation. At the time of writing this book the equivalent price is around £10,000 per acre. When my father was asked why the price of land always seemed to exceed its earning value, his riposte was 'they aren't making any more of it!' In truth, we are losing land in the UK to development, roads, conversion to amenity land, and, in some areas to reforestation.

The picture on a world scale is much more serious. Not only is an increasing volume of land being lost to urbanization – often the best land alongside rivers or the coast, but the Food and Agriculture Organisation (FAO) estimates that 12m hectares (30m acres) of land are lost annually to drought and desertification worldwide[1]. John Steinbeck's book '*The Grapes of Wrath*' vividly describes the human cost of the Dust Bowl years of the 1930's in the Great Plains of the United States. Where once the land had been stabilised by prairie pastures, too much mono-cropping of shallow rooted annual crops resulted in rapid erosion of the topsoil over millions of hectares. Similar problems occurred in northwestern China between 1970-1990, losing billions of tons of valuable soil.

Such losses not only damage the livelihoods of the affected farmers and rural societies, but they severely reduce biodiversity and the ability of the soil to sequester carbon. Preventing losses in the first place is very cost effective when these latter costs are added to the mix, but they are costs not specifically borne by those causing the degradation. Governments need to be proactive in providing appropriate regulatory frameworks to protect the wider interests. All too often this is not the case. There is now a policy of reforestation in China following decades when forests were undervalued for their role in mediating the weather, storing water and carbon, stabilizing the environment and acting as a valuable resource for biodiversity.

By contrast, the extent of deforestation in South East Asia, mainly to plant commercial palm oil plantations in response to Western demand for vegetable oils for consumption and for biofuel, is of great concern. Conservationists point to the loss of some of the most bio-diverse habitats on the planet, whilst the burning and clearance of vast areas of carbon-rich peatland emit significant quantities of $CO_2$. Estimated losses of more than 1 million hectares annually occurred between 2005 and 2015[2]. Scientists point out the hypocrisy of releasing large amounts of greenhouse gases in order to grow crops for Western countries to convert to so-called 'green' fuels. But countries in South East Asia claim this is western self interest to promote home grown biofuels, and that palm oil plantations are vital to growing their young economies. In Africa and South America huge areas of tropical forest have been decimated by illegal logging, slash and burn agriculture and conversion to grazing land to rear livestock. Land use change, which these practices represent, is the biggest single contributor to agricultural emissions of GHG's globally.

The Dust Bowl events in the US and China occurred before we began to see some of the effects of climate change. I noted in chapter 3 that almost 1/3rd cropland in Sub Saharan Africa is degraded and FAO also estimate that up to 20% of African arable land will be less suitable for agriculture by 2080[3] because of these effects. The areas most affected will be those where moisture is already limiting, where so-called dryland agriculture is practised, predominately by smallholders and subsistence farmers. Their livelihoods will be put at severe risk, as will those of many more of the 3 billion people, across the globe, living in such areas, which cover about 40% of the world's surface. The impact of climate change is exacerbated by farming and domestic practices, such as slash and burn agriculture and deforestation (mainly to fuel inefficient heating and cooking systems in poorer societies). Up to 70% of the losses expected by 2030 could be averted through adaptation measures whose economic benefits outweigh the costs[4]. I will speculate later whether economic circumstances, governmental will, social pressures and improved education will enable these changes to take place.

Some climate scientists believe that through better management of our soils and changes to the way we grow crops a great deal of excess carbon in the atmosphere can be sequestered (soaked up) into soil organic matter. Globally soil is a huge carbon sink. Cultivating it releases some of this carbon through oxidation, as I have already noted in the widespread loss of peatland. The idea of using crops to collect atmospheric carbon and lock it into the soil organic matter was put forward by the French delegation at the Climate Change Convention in Paris in 2015. The proposed target was an increase in sequestration rate of carbon by 4 parts per 1000 every year for 20 years. The proposal implicitly accepts that soils have a maximum holding capacity, hence the time limitation, and, because carbon is part of a dynamic cycle of nutrients in living organisms it can be lost as well as captured. On a world scale, assuming the targets were achieved, this would amount to a significant contribution to reducing global warming. Devising ways of paying farmers for sequestering carbon might also be a useful means to support livelihoods, particularly in poorer countries.

But the idea always had its critics. While the '4 per 1000' rate of increase in soil carbon can be achieved in some cases, recent work at Rothamsted Research UK[5] shows this can usually only be achieved with extreme measures that would mainly be impractical or unacceptable. An example would be large annual applications of farmyard manure, which would exceed limits set by the EU and cause significant nitrate pollution. And, of course, sequestration is a one-off process – once the soil has reached its limit it can absorb no more, and any cultivation or disturbance of the soil stimulates carbon release. So it would appear the idea that carbon sequestration can be a major contributor to reducing agriculture's share of global warming is overblown.

The effect of climate change on sea levels will also severely affect the availability of agricultural land, particularly in the longer term. We noted in chapter 2 that the rate of sea level rise is likely to increase over time, severely threatening low lying coastal areas including most of the worlds greatest cities by 2100. Even in the shorter term some coastal land will be inundated, whilst more will be affected by salinisation of groundwater. While this may leave some options for cropping with salt tolerant varieties, the potential for producing food may be severely reduced. Salinisation also occurs widely in warmer climates in areas where groundwater is naturally saline. The worst affected areas are in Australia, Africa and South America. In the drier regions, the removal of tree cover and cropping with shallower rooting crops can raise water table levels, bringing the salts closer to the surface. Where irrigation is practised, particularly using saline groundwater sources, the salt can be deposited in the topsoil layer unless flushed away by further irrigation.

Industrialisation in Britain in the 18th century caused widespread pollution of soils and water. Much of the pollution from modern industry is now highly regulated and controlled. In China, where industrialization is relatively recent, the environment ministry estimates that 16.1% of China's soils exceed State pollution limits[6], particularly by heavy metals, hazardous chemicals and waste. This has implications for human health, crop safety and crop and animal productivity.

Whilst the increase in inorganic fertilizer use has been essential to maintain soil productivity and increase crop yields, there is an environmental cost. By way of example, nitrates are found in drainage water, causing available oxygen in the water to be used up (eutrophication) resulting in loss of biodiversity, toxic algal blooms and dead zones where few fish can survive. The effects extend to estuaries and coastal seas. High nitrate concentrations in drinking water are considered dangerous to human health. Ammonia and oxides of nitrogen are damaging to some plants and can be a threat to human health. Nitrous oxide emitted from soils is a greenhouse gas more potent than carbon dioxide, although it does not survive in the atmosphere for so long. Nitrates can also increase the acidity of soils, and may interact with soil organic matter in ways which are poorly understood. Of the 9 planetary boundaries identified by Rockstrom et al (see previous chapters 2 and 4), the two that have already exceeded safe margins are loss of genetic diversity and excessive nitrate use.

Probably the biggest cause of soil loss worldwide is the result of erosion, either by wind or by water. As rainfall intensity increases, so too does its potential to erode topsoil, particularly on sloping land or land which has little or no vegetative cover. The Foresight Report[7] estimated almost one quarter of all vegetated land on earth (11.5 bn hectares – of which c4.6 bn is cropped) has undergone some form of human induced soil degradation, the majority of which is through erosion and the loss of organic matter.

An ideal soil would probably consist of 45% minerals, 25% water, 25% air and 5% organic matter. This 5% fraction nevertheless is critically important, yet poorly understood. About 60% of it is carbon, derived from the breakdown of living organisms. In chapter 3 I noted that the soil is a vast repository of carbon, and can either act as a potential storehouse through carbon sequestration or an emitter of greenhouse gases (both $CO_2$ and $N_2O$) on a vast scale. So the management of soil fertility, particularly carbon, is essential for maintaining agricultural productivity, reducing risk of failure, helping reduce the causal agents of climate change and improving the resilience of agricultural systems to changing climate.

Modern farming systems have often fallen short of good soil management practice. There are many complex reasons why 'good stewardship' has, and continues to be compromised. The UK experience demonstrates some of the pressures on farmers, shared to a greater or lesser extent by farmers around the world. Farming has always been a risky business. Unlike many industrial processes the fortunes of a farmer depend much more on the vagaries of the weather and the uncertainties faced by every living organism such as disease, malnutrition or genetic malfunction. Experts are deeply concerned that climate change will further exacerbate these risks. But economic uncertainties add another layer of risk, making farming returns unusually volatile, and profits are often very small in relation to the capital employed within the business. I will discuss risk, volatility and investment in a later chapter, but note, for now, that while many governments recognize the peculiar situation of farmers and offer a variety of support measures to assist them, their main political concern is to ensure that consumers have adequate access to cheap food. My father told me, when I first began farming, that I would prosper when the market was 'short'. In other words, when prices were forced upwards by excess demand over supply. For politicians that scenario is anathema, because it leads to a disgruntled electorate, which has come to expect, in recent years, that food will always be cheap and plentiful.

Despite severe economic pressures on producers most of the time, successful farmers have kept their heads above water by adopting new technologies to reduce costs and increase yields. The cost of labour, in particular, has been reduced dramatically in my lifetime. In 1970, when I began farming, I employed 10 full-time men on 700 acres. Twenty years earlier my father employed a similar number on half that acreage. By the time I handed over the farm to my nephew I had 6 men on 1500 acres, but half of these were employed on a much expanded livestock enterprise. That enterprise was sold when I retired and the same 1500 acres now employ no full-time staff and only one or two contract and seasonal workers. This has been achieved by mechanisation and specialisation.

The capacity of new machines while allowing much more work to be done with fewer people, requires rationalization of the 'factory floor' to work optimally. This means bigger fields and greater aggregation of mono-cropping within a given area. Both trends have an impact on the wildlife and biodiversity of the farm, which may only partially be replaced by dedicated 'wildlife areas' encouraged by conservationists and governments. Concerns over disturbance to the 'balance of nature' together with worries about the long-term effects of 'chemical farming' on human health, the environment and on soils give rise to advocacy of organic farming, which I will discuss in more depth later in the book.

As machines increase in size and complexity their effect on the structure of the soil can be harmful. Current concerns over an apparent plateau in the trend of rising average crop yields stem partly from reduced expenditure on varietal research but also from likely structural damage to soils from heavy machinery. The complexity of the soil environment makes work on this problem difficult and long-term, but we do know that average organic matter in UK soils has reduced to a level of 3% to 3.5%, with many areas below this figure, particularly where mixed arable and livestock farming has largely given way to specialist crop production.

Economic pressures on farmers can be shown to affect their decisions on maintaining the long-term fertility of the soil. Most soils contain adequate 'buffer' stocks of phosphate and potash, the nutrients next in importance to nitrates for plant growth. Since the turn of the millennium in the UK there has typically been a 30% reduction in annual applications of these key nutrients[8] leading to a potentially serious rundown in reserves of those nutrients. At the same time, because of the pressures to specialize and to maximize the acreage of the most profitable crops, nature is fighting back with an increase in herbicide resistant weeds and a range of plant diseases mutating more quickly. This may force some farmers to consider reintroducing a more traditional rotational system of cropping and a wider range of crop types, in order to regain control.

Meanwhile, as we learn more about the effects of the more traditional forms of cultivation, such as ploughing, which can seriously reduce valuable wildlife in the soil, damage structure and release greenhouse gases to the atmosphere, there is pressure on farmers to change their systems. A UK Parliamentary select Committee in 2016[9] concluded that farmland soils must be better protected for future generations. As always with soil, this is not straightforward, or cheap. A great many academic studies laud the practices of minimum tillage, often coupled with out of season cover cropping, but many farmers recognize the risks of using these techniques when they may not be appropriate to the specific weather and soil conditions at the time of drilling. Good stewardship is not always easy to define! In many tropical countries, where soils may be more fragile and rainfall events more violent, the argument is stronger for reduced tillage and planting of cover crops in order to prevent erosion or to retain soil moisture for longer.

Similar economic pressures on farmers apply the world over, leading to short-term decision making, either with a view to making a financial return, or, in the case of millions of smallholder farmers, trying to survive until the next harvest. In many countries this short-termism is exacerbated by poorly regulated, often unfair and insecure systems of land tenure, which offer no incentive to farmers, with few resources, to care for the land for the longer term.

Women in agriculture in the UK are a relatively new phenomenon. In many less developed countries women are the backbone of farming. It is women who perform much of the manual labour but often they are not legally recognized as landholders and are not offered technical or economic advice to help them run their farms. A significant part of the solution to raising agricultural productivity, in Africa in particular, depends on improving the legal status of women farmers and providing them with credit and advisory services to help them use existing technology more effectively and to adopt new techniques and new crops appropriate to their local situations.

We need to look at the challenges implicit in moving relatively backward areas of world agriculture toward a more productive future, whilst taking care not to upset further the natural balance of nature on which we all depend. At the same time there is evidently much to do to set western style agriculture on a sustainable path for the future. So the next chapter considers the current status and direction of agricultural research, the technologies available, potential pitfalls and problems and whether research can really be translated into widespread farm practice.

# Chapter 6

# Research and Technology

'We live in a society exquisitely dependent on science and technology, in which hardly anyone knows anything about science and technology.'

*(Carl Sagan)*

One of the most concerning trends in the last few years has been an increase in both public and political derision of scientific data when that data does not conform to preferred beliefs or interests. A prime example is Donald Trumps' denial of the importance of climate change. I mentioned earlier, a similar scepticism by Lord Lawson as an example of a body of predominantly right wing thinking in the UK, where loathing of the prospect of 'more government' appears to colour attitudes to the vast weight of scientific opinion. In Europe the rejection by many countries of GMO (Genetically Modified Organisms) technology and continuing argument over the re-licensing of the herbicide glyphosate appears to be associated with a visceral hatred of corporate capitalism and the strength of so called 'green' lobbyists.

Yet I can also cite instances where science has been found wanting. I was a young man when Rachel Carson's book, *Silent Spring*[1] was published in the US. It was a wake up call to the unforseen dangers of using organo-chlorine pesticides widely in the environment. Because these chemicals failed to degrade sufficiently, animals and birds higher up the food chain built up increasingly toxic levels in their bodies, leading to severely reduced populations of raptor species in particular and complete individual species loss in some geographic areas. In the following years we have developed sophisticated safety protocols around farm chemicals to reassure the public, but that does not preclude misuse or the occasional mistake. I have seen toxic chemicals being used in both India and Africa with little regard for risk to operator or the environment. Manufacturers sometimes do not pick up sufficient data in their trials to identify problems which then occur in the field. It is possible that the effects of neonicotenoids on insect pollinators were underestimated, and that severe declines in the numbers of these species may be related. A recent study in Germany[2] showed general insect populations had declined by 75% in 30 years. Major pesticide companies claimed that cause and effect could not be identified, but in a debate in the European Parliament the report author said that *'not knowing the exact cause should not be an excuse to do nothing'*. Such cases give some credibility to those who claim the 'precautionary principle' should always prevail, even though the implication that we should take no risks would have precluded huge swathes of beneficial innovation and human progress.

Often the science is good, but the way that the resulting technology is used causes problems. With all things natural there is an inherent resilience; nature fights back. We see this in the development of pesticide resistance which often arises quite quickly if a particular pesticide is used too widely or frequently. Overuse of glyphosate (trademark name Roundup) has led to resistant weeds occurring in more than half of the states in the US, with Brazil following close behind. In both cases the worst infestations are in areas where so called 'Roundup ready' crops are widely grown, that is those varieties which have inbred resistance to the herbicide which kills all other green plants. In the same way, antibiotic resistance is a growing and major concern to human health, largely exacerbated by over prescribing by doctors and misuse by patients, but also by unecessarily widespread use in animal husbandry, not just for treating individuals for disease but for group therapy, and for growth promotion. In the UK livestock farmers are generally pretty good at minimising antibiotic use, and certainly do not use them for growth promotion. Across the world, however, there continues to be widespread and indiscriminate use both in animal and human medicine. In 2013 Reuters[3] and the state-backed news website ThePaper.cn reported that China used around half the world's total volume of antibiotics. It added that more than 50,000 tons of antibiotics were discharged into China's waterways and soil. In the animal sector a report from the Centre for Disease Dynamics, Economics and Policy[4] stated that 64,000 tons were used currently, and that level is expected to rise to c105,000 tons by 2030. In the US, about 80% of antibiotics are used for livestock and 20% for humans. Because of international trade and travel a problem of antibiotic resistance in one country can quickly become a global one.

All of this preamble serves to put into context the likely direction of science and technology around agriculture and food in the next few years. Across the world government-backed agricultural advisory services, together with research work to back them up, were cut severely from the 1980's, until recently. Created largely in response to food shortages in times of war, they were seen as unnecessarily generous in times of surplus. The Green Revolution in Asia enabled the most populous countries to produce sufficient food to sustain their peoples, and although poverty and hunger tragically remain in many areas of the world, this is due to lack of access to food rather than lack of food per se. In the West, following the surplus production which built up from the 1970's and 1980's, politicians sought to mitigate the increasing costs of surplus storage or disposal by cutting back government subsidies for farm production, and also support for research and development. It is difficult, once an infrastructure has been broken, to rebuild it quickly, and even though there is growing acceptance that the rate of progress in developing agriculture needs to increase to meet the challenges outlined in this book, that change is slow. In Africa, where the green revolution made little impact, and where population and demand for food is now growing rapidly, many countries suffer from weak or corrupt governance and shortage of funds to invest in research and development. Often, funding has been prioritized to other industries and to 'vanity' projects, and despite pan African agreement to raise the share of spending on agriculture to 10% of countries' GDP[5] (Gross Domestic Product), the majority of countries still have some way to go to reach that figure. A 2014 report on behalf of IFPRI (International Food Policy Research Institute)[6] found that R & D spending in most of Sub Saharan Africa has not kept pace with growth in agricultural output. There were not enough researchers, particularly senior ones; significant knowledge gaps were evident; funding was skewed toward short term returns and was highly dependent on donors and development banks, and was often unpredictable. Unlike developed economies, private sector investment was very limited and represented a significant untapped resource.

Nevertheless as Governments have become more aware of potential shortages of food in the future, as a consequence of climate change and increasing environmental damage, many have reviewed their attitude to investment in science and technology in the sector. This has coincided with a revolution in crop and animal breeding techniques leading to quicker introduction of new varieties of crops and breeds of animals. Together with the availability of extensive monitoring equipment and affordable data processing, precision technologies in both animal and crop farming are in a period of rapid development in wealthier countries. Against the backdrop of hugely heightened environmental concerns over the damage that agriculture has done, and continues to do to the natural world, a new word has entered the political and agricultural lexicon – 'sustainability'.

Sustainability is a slippery word, meaning different things to different groups of people. To farmers it primarily means a system of running their businesses to take account of environmental concerns but allowing them to make a reasonable living from their work and investment. To environmentalists the term implies a neutral, or close to neutral effect on the natural resources used by agriculture. Greta Thunberg, the 16 year old climate change activist, suggests that our response cannot be *a little bit sustainable*, analogous to the saying that you cannot be 'a little bit pregnant'. Recognising that farming is at root exploitative, in producing food which is then consumed off the farm, the environmentalists ideal would be to achieve as near to a 'circular economy' as possible, with a return of waste products to the soil, and a minimum use of externally sourced inputs such as artificial fertiliser. Some criticise the term because it fails to address sustainability issues such as access to food by the poorest people, or its equitable distribution. To Governments it means 'producing more for less' to meet increasing demand at affordable prices whilst using less fertiliser and sprays.

Of course this gives rise to interminable debate over what should be the 'true' definition. What should be a 'meeting point' between agriculturalists and environmentalists all too easily becomes a major point of dispute. The arguments are exacerbated when we add another hotly contested word, 'intensification'. 'Sustainable intensification' has been widely adopted as the appropriate way forward for the agricultural sector, because it appears to reflect the requirement for more food as populations grow and diets change with improving lifestyles, alongside the need to minimise environmental damage. The term was originally coined by Prof. Jules Pretty (1997) but came to prominence in a significant body of work commissioned by the UK Government Office for Science Foresight project on *Global Food and Farming Futures'2010'*, led by Prof. Charles Godfray. It examined in detail the growing demand for food worldwide, future trends in the supply of food, the potential effects of climate change and competition for resources, such as water, and a number of 'cross-cutting' themes, such as subsidy regimes, price volatility and governance of food systems, which all impact on the ability of the population to feed itself. The study came to the relatively optimistic conclusion that '*major advances in sustainable food production and availability can be achieved with the concerted application of current technologies (given sufficient political will), and the importance of investing in research sooner rather than later to enable the food system to cope with both known and unknown challenges in the coming decades*[8].' The conclusion was based on the premise that new techniques would need to be developed in agriculture to reduce chemical inputs and environmental damage, but critically, to enable agricultural yields to rise sufficiently to meet increasing demand for food.

In consequence, most agricultural research in developed countries is now directed toward increasing productivity at lower environmental cost. Technology is aimed at increasing precision, identifying and dealing with problems and processes, so as to reduce cost and damage to the environment. There is good reason to examine diverse approaches to achieve these goals including conventional, high-tech, agro-ecological and organic techniques, because all systems have something to offer, and different approaches will suit different regions and circumstances. Neither should we discount the more novel technologies such as hydroponics (non-soil production of crops), 'artificial meat' manufacture, or farming insects for protein.

Throughout my working career farming in the UK the vast majority of research has been on increasing crop yield and animal productivity. That understandably remains the mindset of most researchers and farmers. Governments have generally been supportive of an industry which provides the general public with good food at prices which represent a decreasing share of average income. Immediately after World War II food was scarce and farmers received generous subsidies to encourage greater production, helped by new technologies which greatly increased the potential for higher yields. Within 30 years farmers in wealthy countries were producing embarrassingly large surpluses of grain, milk and wine. Government support was trimmed back and began to reflect other concerns over environmental damage and food safety. But the emphasis of research remained on productivity gains, because that seemed the only way to increase farming profits as farmgate prices fell and a bigger share of

41

consumers food expenditure was grabbed beyond the farm gate by processors and retailers.

In most developed economies there is increasing demand from pressure groups and the general public for governments to make agriculture 'greener'. I will examine this in more detail in the next chapter, but here it is worth rehearsing an argument not often heard in farming circles, but relevant to the changing direction of agricultural research in these countries. I have been discussing food security thus far as if consumers in wealthy countries face imminent shortage. That is far from the truth. In fact, consumers are presented with a bigger range of products at relatively affordable prices than ever before in history. I will discuss the different situation in many poorer countries later, but for now it is evident that there is a 'disconnect' between the market farmers currently serve in order to survive economically, and the future global scenario I described earlier in this book.

In 2014 Professor Alan Buckwell published an essay[9] on food security which questioned the conventional wisdom of increasing production to meet ever increasing demand. In it he suggested that growth in global population had become a *'convenient shorthand which is taken implicitly to justify the protection of EU agriculture'*. But European populations are not increasing much at all, and are expected to peak around 2030, then slowly decline. *'It was in the context of the challenge especially facing the developing countries that the term sustainable intensification emerged to describe the necessary development path of agriculture'*. So what should this phrase mean when applied to developed country agriculture? Buckwell goes on to suggest that the emphasis here should be more on the word 'sustainable' than on 'intensification'. The Biotechnology and Biological Sciences Research Council (BBSRC)) takes the view that each word should have similar weight. This is reflected in the research strategy 2017–2022 of Rothamsted Research Station, part of BBSRC. The work centres on breeding superior crops, including yield, quality and efficiency of resource use, and discovering novel traits to improve the nutritional or industrial value of plants, securing productivity through better monitoring of pests and diseases together with development of 'smart' crop protection strategies, and improving future agri-food systems by closing the yield gap between potential and actual average farm yield, and creating crop and livestock systems with higher performance and nutrient value but lower environmental impact. BBSRC are also examining improving technologies such as robotics, smart sensors, drones, and 'vertical farming' techniques (hydroponic crop production in 'factory' environments using no soil).

There is a wide range of work by other institutes and by farmers themselves which indicates a change in emphasis from 'all out yield' to a more balanced approach giving consideration to issues such as protecting the environment and to public concerns over pesticide use, loss of biodiversity and animal welfare. John Chinn, Chair of the Centre for Crop Health and Protection forecast, in an article in Farmer's Weekly[10] what farming in the UK might look like by 2030. He visualises much lower quantity of agrochemical use as a result of spraying targeted plants only, and greater use of biological control. No-till or minimum tillage systems of cultivation could become the norm, together with greater use of companion and cover crops, all designed to enhance soil structure and reduce nutrient loss. 'Big Data' and improved diagnostics could forecast and deal with pests and diseases before they become problematical and spot incipient problems with plant nutrition or water availability. He proposes a similar list for animal husbandry.

For many years I was Chairman of a farmer owned research centre, and I still remain on the Board of Trustees. During the latter half of the last century most of our work entailed providing farmers with specific advice on agrochemical use. But early on in the current century we have switched to longer term projects examining rotational effects, cover cropping, different tillage techniques and greater examination of soil biology. In some trials we are looking at mixing organic farming principles with limited agrochemical use.

Organic farming precludes the use of almost all agrochemicals and, more recently the Soil Association, the certifying authority in the UK for organic farmers, has proscribed genetically modified organisms (GMO's) as well as crops derived from more recent techniques such as CRISPR-cas9 gene editing. The European Court of Justice gave a long awaited verdict on this technique on 25th July 2018, siding with the environmental activists and severely disappointing the EU biotech industry. There is an uneasy relationship between many 'conventional' farmers and some organic farmers because some conventional techniques as well as potentially valuable scientifically innovative techniques are condemned as environmentally and morally 'bad' by the organic lobby. That is a pity, because we have much to learn from each other, but that requires a less ideological approach than is often taken.

It is sometimes argued[11] that organic agriculture could feed the world whilst reducing both nitrogen and pesticide use very substantially and with significant benefits to wildlife and human health. Because organic yields are necessarily lower than those in conventional agriculture this implies the need for greater areas of land for similar overall production. It can, therefore, be argued that greater land use leads to more environmental damage and increased greenhouse gas emissions. Muller counters this by suggesting that no extra land use would be required if widespread organic production were associated with reduced meat and milk consumption, together with reduced food waste. It should be noted that Muller, quite properly suggests that in the absence of livestock it would be challenging to maintain an adequate supply of nitrogen to maintain yields. More recently Professor of Environmental Science at Cambridge University, Andrew Balmford, published a study supporting the argument that reserving sufficient land for wildlife, and intensifying production on the remainder makes the most environmental sense, given that sufficient food must be produced to satisfy consumer needs. Taken together, these two points of view are examples of an ongoing 'land sharing' versus 'land sparing' debate.

While nitrogen is an essential nutrient for crop growth, the majority of nitrogen applied to crops is manufactured in a process which uses around 7% of all man made energy. Without this inorganic form of nitrogen it is estimated that 40% of the human race would not have adequate food supply[13]. But because it is so widely used in agriculture, a significant portion is lost in solution in rainwater leaching through the soil profile and through loss to the air, principally as nitrous oxide. Nitrous oxide ($N_2O$) is another greenhouse gas with a shorter life in the atmosphere than $CO_2$, but with a warming capacity 293 times greater. That portion of nitrate lost to groundwater is damaging to aquatic life causing algal bloom in waterways, which has become a major problem worldwide. Excess nitrates and nitrites in drinking water can also be damaging to human health. I noted earlier that one of the two 'global boundaries' already crossed is that of nitrate use. So it is no surprise that, despite its enormous value as a plant nutrient, an EU scientific report, in 2011[14] estimated the costs of dealing with the problems caused by it in Europe at <u>more</u> than its value to agriculture. The report argued for greater public awareness, perhaps through the publication of nitrogen 'footprints' for different products, and noted that there are substantial health benefits to be gained by '*keeping consumption of animal products within recommended dietary limits*'. Reducing meat and milk consumption and production by 50% could lead to a 37-40% decrease in EU agricultural reactive nitrogen emissions and reduce the requirement for imported soybeans for animal feed by 75%[15]. I will have a good deal more to say about this in later chapters.

There is probably more public disquiet about pesticide use in agriculture than anything else, (excepting, perhaps, animal welfare). I have always found it odd that most people are willing to swallow endless chemicals in the form of 'medicines' whilst criticising farmers because minute traces of chemicals from crop spraying can sometimes be detected on foodstuffs. It is difficult to make many people understand that a poison is only a poison if the dose is high enough. Water can kill if you drink it to excess. Food itself is comprised of chemicals, some of which at inappropriate levels of consumption can be harmful. American research[16], reported in the 'Economist' (March 3rd 2018), show that pesticides can change the nutritional value of some crops, which could be beneficial in some cases, but perhaps not in others. Nevertheless, as I have explained, some agrochemicals have caused problems in the environment and, sometimes, these problems have not become evident soon enough, despite rigorous testing regulations imposed on manufacturers by governments. In Europe the approximate cost of meeting these regulations is around €200m per chemical, and rising. No wonder, then that the pipeline of new products is drying up, and that manufacturers are only interested in investing where sales potential is high enough to see a financial return. That generally means minor crops grown on relatively small areas get very little agrochemical innovation. In the National Institute for Agricultural Botany (NIAB) magazine, agronomist Bill Clark, suggests that proposed EU regulations could see 35%-45% loss of crop protection products for farmer use by 2020[17]. Fewer products with different modes of action available to combat weeds and pests encourages farmers to over use what is available, and this, of course, leads to faster development of resistant organisms. In NIAB's Agri-Environment notes[17] in Nov. 2017, the case is made for a standard testing regime which mirrors that of pharmaceuticals. Currently the toxicity tests carried out on pesticides to gain approval rely on a limited number of test species, leaving questions as to their applicability in the wider environment. Whilst pharmaceuticals have significant safety trials before release they also have a system of feedback of negative effects once they have been released for general use. Pesticides do not have such a formal monitoring system, and although a very precautionary approach is given to issuing licences for use in the first place, a product can continue to be used in compliance with the label for the period of the licence. Perhaps a monitoring system, now much easier to conceive with the emergence of 'big data', could help change negative consumer attitudes to pesticides. Alongside inorganic nitrogen they remain vital to current and foreseeable systems of food production.

So many of the chemicals used in conventional farming are under pressure as environmental considerations gain ascendency in the public and political mind. The challenge to increase yields whilst using less fertiliser and sprays is huge, and considerable hope is currently vested in new breeding techniques for plants and animals, which might allow scientists to develop more quickly and more precisely new plant varieties and breeds of animals which are more resistant to disease or capable of high yields without the need for excessive inputs. A range of novel techniques have revolutionised the science of breeding in recent years. Perhaps most significant is the ability to sequence the genetic code of crops and animals at relatively low cost. This allows easier identification of genes responsible for certain characteristics, which can then be used to select more accurately potentially useful crosses. Whilst speeding up conventional breeding methods it can also opens the way to other molecular techniques, the first of which was GM (genetic modification) technology. The widespread use of GM crops around the world has been highly controversial, partly because of the way in which the technique was first employed by one large US company seeking to maximise the use of the agrochemical glyphosate ('Roundup'), which it also manufactured. A mixture of concern over the power and intentions of 'big business' coupled with worries that the technique involved transference of genes between different species, with potentially unknowable outcomes from further natural crossings in the wider environment, combined to produce a massive public backlash.

In 2015 more than half the EU 28 member states decided to ban GM crops, despite their being widely grown in many other parts of the world. Properly used and regulated, the technique has enormous potential for good, for instance in creating crop varieties able to tolerate drought or soil salinity, genetic traits which are badly needed in some areas of the world. Alternatively, since c.29% of people worldwide suffer from micronutrient deficiency[19], such as zinc, iron or Vitamin B, crops could be developed with enhanced levels of these nutrients. Sadly, much of this potential is stalled because of public concerns, particularly in Europe, and despite the fact that new varieties would have great benefit for them, many African countries have followed Europe's lead. The traditional model of GM as a tool by which big transnational companies can dominate the world is now patently untrue. At an FAO symposium on agricultural biotechnology in 2016[20] it was clear that many other developing countries around the world are now researching their own biotech crops, often in public/private partnerships. Some technologies are less subject to intellectual property rights restrictions and are, therefore, widely available and relatively cheap.

A step on from GM technology is GE (gene editing), which does not implant genes from foreign species but effectively offers a much faster method of breeding than normal crossing and selection techniques (mutagenesis). In simple terms this technique uses a pair of 'genetic scissors' to snip out or insert genes within the plant genome. The result is effectively the same as might be achieved by mutagenesis, but in much shorter time and with more accuracy. The most widely known technique of this kind is called CRISPR-cas9. Because of the uproar over GM the European court in 2018 ruled that the technique cannot be used in the EU, although this ruling is being challenged by several member countries. As I indicated earlier, the organic certification body for the UK, the Soil Association, currently refuses to recognise varieties produced in this way. It seems perverse to discount a technology which offers such potential to reduce concerns over other areas of modern agricultural practice, such as pesticides and excess use of nitrogen. Such varieties are already in production in other parts of the world and I hope that common sense will prevail in the corridors of power in Europe.

So far I have reflected a mainly UK and EU centric view of the problems and challenges which researchers and farmers are facing. The need for enhanced productivity in food supply is greater in poorer countries than in rich ones. It is in these nations that the population is growing fastest, and where there is most need for a greater supply of food and greater equity of distribution of what is available. In countries which are in transition from poverty to relative affluence, we see the results of the inequity of affordable supply in dietary changes conducive to obesity, and which pose real problems of public health. I will devote a whole chapter to food and health, because it forms a vital link in the argument this book makes for an holistic solution to the challenge of 'future food'.

Let me first consider the situation of Sub Saharan Africa (SSA), where future population increases are greatest and where poverty is most widespread. The late Calestous Juma, author of a widely praised book on

African agriculture, (*The New Harvest – Agricultural innovation in Africa*[21]), suggested that 75% of African farmland is starved of nutrients. Fertiliser use is 10% of world average and less that 3% of total cropland is under sustainable land and water management. The Montpelier Panel of experts[22], of which Juma was a member, estimated that 26% (and rising) of the region constitutes a hotspot for land degradation. This can be seen graphically in maps published by the Panel showing the extensive areas where highly weathered acid soils, and aluminium toxicity in particular, restrict crop yields dramatically.

More than 50% of Africa's population lives in arid, semi-arid or dry sub-humid areas. This currently amounts to some 600m people across 75% of the total land area[23]. In much of this area it is difficult to provide sufficient food to eat, let alone increase income from agriculture. And climate change in these regions is predicted to reduce the length of growing periods (when there is sufficient moisture and low enough temperatures for crop growth). Typically farmers crop 0.5 – 3.0 ha of land to support their family, under constant threat of bad weather or of pests destroying their meagre crops.

And yet, Africa grows a vast range of indigenous crops, many adapted to the harsh conditions. The continent contains probably 60% of the world's available arable land[24] although further encroachment into its natural habitats poses a major threat to biodiversity. In many areas there is adequate fresh water for irrigation if appropriate infrastructure can be provided. There is potential for Africa to feed itself, and even be a major food exporter if sufficient investment in markets, transport and storage infrastructure is made. This would also require widespread availability of plant nutrients, sources of finance and reformed land tenure systems giving confidence to farmers to invest.

Globally more than 6000 species have been cultivated for food, yet fewer than 200 make major contributions to food production today, and only 9 account for 66% of total crop production[25]. Similar statistics are reported for animal species used for food. The world is only slowly waking up to the inherent risks in not widening research and investment into a greater diversity of food sources.

In order to encourage farmers to exploit this potential, research and development (R&D) specific to local needs is vital. Some technology developed in different parts of the world may be appropriate to transfer to new areas, but more technical development is often needed to reflect local soil and climatic conditions, social norms, dietary preferences and changing climate, (which is happening faster in the tropics than in most other areas). The World Bank predicts climate change could slightly enhance crop yields in temperate and cool regions of the world, but the tropics could suffer 20-50% yield reduction by 2050[26] if no changes are made to existing systems of production.

In some of the more arid areas, livestock farming is fundamental to pastoral livelihoods. Improved management systems, new grass varieties offering better nutritional traits, tolerance of extreme conditions and pest resistance, would help. What is also evident, though, is that research is of little use unless it is taken up and used. Farmers the world over are generally 'conservative' in adopting new techniques. In commercial farming, where my experience lies, new ideas tend to attract the 'early adopters', who may, sometimes steal a march on their fellow farmers, but often fail. So the majority tends to take time before committing itself to increased risk. In other industries the outcome of new technologies is usually more predictable, but in farming each field can react differently each season and what works in one year may not work the next. In less developed countries where risk of failure is greater, and where many have no other resources to fall back on should failure occur, it is inevitable that farmers will be extremely cautious in shouldering more risk for uncertain reward.

Education and finance are both essential to translate research into practice. As Howard Buffett, President of the Howard G. Buffett Foundation says[27], '*Without a biologically based, sustainable soil fertility plan combined with education and training, and, most important, a serious and long term commitment from Government, seeds and fertiliser alone will not succeed.*' The members of the Montpelier Panel[28] concur, and recommend investment in effective farm extension services to educate farmers on the best farming practices for local conditions. It is likely that this will be a mix of traditional knowledge and new technology. In China, where considerable progress in transforming the agricultural sector has been made in recent years, Vice Agriculture Minister Ye Zhenquin announced that China intends to train more than 1 million new 'professional' farmers in 2018 for the development of modern agriculture in the country, stressing the need for effective translation of R&D into farm practice[29].

There is a lot to play for in terms of raising yields. A number of studies analyse the 'yield gap' between potential yield and average farm yield for different crops in different regions of the world. Perhaps the most comprehensive study published to date is from the Australian government run

Australian Centre for International Agricultural Research[30]. Worldwide, for wheat the average yield gap was 48%, for rice 76% and for maize 104%. These global figures mask a huge variation in regional averages. Taking maize as an example, in 2010 estimated potential yield (PY) in Iowa, USA was 15 tonnes/ha with average farm yield (FY) at 11.4 tonnes, a yield gap of 36%. For Ukraine, PY was 12 tonnes with FY at 4.4 tonnes, a gap of 170%. For Western Africa, PY was 5.3 tonnes and FY at 1.7 tonnes, a gap of 200%. We do not grow grain maize commercially in the UK, but wheat is a major crop and even here the yield gap was calculated at 34%, with the gap of the best performing region, Northern France, at 26%. The potential to grow more with existing technology, if only farmers could exploit it fully, is clearly huge. Research may not translate into practice for many reasons, including the level of farmer knowledge about research findings.

Investment in both R&D and knowledge transfer by national governments is essential as farming conditions change. India has the largest cultivated land mass in the world at 170m ha. 55% of the population is engaged in agriculture and average farm size is only half what it was 40 years ago[31]. Agriculture in that country faces a very challenging future. The Indian Government estimates that 60% of agricultural land is at risk because of fertiliser misuse, poor cropping practices and soil nutrient deficiencies. In addition, India uses 13% of total world extracted water of which 87% is used for irrigation. Aquifers, particularly in the north of the country are exploited at unsustainable rates. Water levels are decreasing at a rate of 33cm per year, making it increasingly costly and difficult to pump supplies.The likelihood is that climate change will lead to declining monsoon rains. Another effect of global warming is the shrinking of Himalayan glaciers, which may, in the short term lead to greater river flow (and potential flooding), but in the longer term to shortages as the volume of snow meltwater decreases.

Investment by the Indian Government in agricultural R&D is c0.4% of agricultural Gross Domestic Product. In developing countries a generally accepted target level is 1.0%. Private sector investment in research is low at 17% of the total. The Green Revolution of the 1980's transformed India's agriculture and enabled the country to feed its huge population, but agricultural productivity has stalled and demand for food is outstripping ability to supply, particularly in the breadbasket areas of the North which rely heavily on irrigation. Unlike many countries in Africa, India possesses an enormous pool of agricultural specialists and entrepreneurs and a good education system. It should be well positioned to turn the challenges it faces into opportunities for agricultural growth, but it needs good leadership and greater investment in the sector.

Let me turn finally in this chapter to consider China, where there are more than 200m farmers despite the industrial revolution that has transformed the country in the last 40 years. Since the major policy reforms of 1978, production of China's main food commodities has increased eightfold, with production of meat and vegetables topping the list[32]. The country has certainly invested in R&D and new technologies enabling it to feed most of its enormous population and to cope with significant changes in consumer diets which now contain a higher proportion of 'resource hungry' meat and milk products.

I noted above the recent Chinese government initiatives to invest heavily in educating farmers (known as 'extension'). Part of the rationale behind this lies in the need to use technology appropriately. Chinese farmers have certainly increased their productivity, but at very considerable environmental cost, with major implications for future sustainability and quality of life. To some extent the situation reflects the position that faced UK and EU agriculture some 30 years ago. China now has huge problems with water quality resulting from pollution, particularly by excessive use of nitrogen fertilisers, but also from animal wastes and agrochemicals. Despite noting these problems, none of the post 2006 five year plans have addressed them. Recent proposals by government include training, better labelling of fertilisers, spatial planning of intensive livestock units, and standards for waste disposal, storage of manures as well as payments to farmers for ecosystem services and reducing perverse subsidies on fertilisers which encouraged overuse. It will be interesting to monitor the effects of these proposals given that, as Scott Rozelle, China expert of Stanford University said in National Geographic Magazine, *'The vast number of small farms makes China's food system almost completely unmanageable in terms of food safety'*. It might also make it very difficult for Chinese bureaucrats to control environmental damage. The next chapter considers the environmental effects of agriculture and food in more detail.

# Chapter 7

# Environment

'We cannot manage what we do not measure'

*(The economics of ecosystems and biodiversity (TEEB) for agriculture and food, UNEP, 2016, p.xi)*

As a boy in the 1950's I remember walking along a green lane at Easter, picking my mother a mixed posy of wild flowers from the hedgerow. Even then most of the meadows no longer contained the rich mix of species that were common 20 years before. Today, it is rare in my part of East Anglia around Easter to see anything other than primroses and cowslips, where once there would have been ten or twenty species of flowering plants in profusion. And in my part of Norfolk I have not heard a cuckoo calling for at least five years.

In September 2016 a consortium of UK conservation and research organisations launched its report[1] '*State of Nature 2016*' at the Royal Society in London. It showed that between 1970 and 2013, 56% of almost 4000 species studied had declined, with 40% showing strong or moderate declines. Over the same period 44% of species increased with 29% showing strong or moderate increases. In apportioning responsibility for such dramatic changes the report pointed the finger strongly at '*policy driven agricultural change*'. The following month saw the publication of '*The Living Planet Report 2016*' by WWF[2] and the Zoological Society of London, which showed that overall terrestrial species of mammals, birds, amphibians and reptiles found in habitats ranging from grasslands to forests have seen populations decline by 38% since 1970. Freshwater species, including fish have declined by a dramatic 81%. Meanwhile a study by Kew Gardens[3] revealed that at least one in five of all plant species are endangered. Of these, almost one third are threatened by agricultural activities, through monoculture plantations (e.g. for palm oil or rubber) and animal grazing, deforestation, invasive species, environmental changes (including fires), agricultural chemicals and climate change (especially in mountainous areas).

Mention was made in the previous chapter of the catastrophic decline in insect numbers as instanced by a study in Germany showing 75% decline in 30 years, described by some as 'ecological Armageddon'. Another report carried by the journal Science Advances[4] suggests that more than 7% of Earth's natural intact forest landscapes have been lost since 2000, and these ecosystems may be in danger of disappearing entirely from at least 19 countries in the next 60 years. Intact forest landscapes, by virtue of their size and pristine condition, can provide crucial habitat for all kinds of wildlife. Many of them are also significant carbon 'sinks', making them important for global climate mitigation, and these are the forest landscapes most at risk from destruction.

The World Economic Forum *2018 Global Risks Report*[5] shows that environmental risks have grown in prominence over the 13 year history of the Report. All 5 risks identified in this category are believed to be increasing in both perceived likelihood and impact. They are extreme weather events and temperatures, accelerating biodiversity loss, pollution of air, soil and water, failures of climate change mitigation and adaptation, and transition risks as we move to a low carbon future. (The last risk foresees economic and social upheaval resulting from fossil fuel divestment and large scale labour disruption). The Report states these environmental risks are exacerbated by risks in other categories such as water crises and involuntary migration of people displaced by economic stringency and climate change.

Since over 75% of the world's food is derived from just 12 plant and 5 animal species there is increasing risk of catastrophic breakdown in the food system. With increased severe weather events resulting from climate warming the Food and Agriculture Organisation of the UN (FAO) predict a one in twenty chance per decade of simultaneous failure of maize production in the world's two main growing areas, China and the United States[6ibid]. This would cause widespread famine and hardship. In 2017 $CO_2$ emissions began rising again after 4 years of stability, and passed the 400 parts per million mark, compared to a pre industrial baseline of 280ppm. Trends appear to be upward again, and studies suggest that the oceans ability to absorb more $CO_2$ may be declining. It is believed they have absorbed 93% of global temperature rise between 1971 and 2010.

The changes I have seen in my environment in my lifetime, are, in microcosm, the kind of changes which have happened worldwide. Indeed, as I have explained, there are vast areas of the world where much greater environmental damage has occurred, and often in a shorter time span. This gives us pause to consider whether our headlong race for 'better lives' is selfish indulgence at best and hugely irresponsible at worst. I will consider this later in this chapter and elsewhere in the book.

The Intergovernmental Science Policy Platform on Biodiversity and Ecosystem Services (IPBES), which has 129 State members, published an authoritative report[7], confirming the urgency of reducing and reversing land degradation to protect biodiversity and the ecosystem services vital to all life on earth. These problems are already affecting the lives of 3.2 billion people and pushing the planet towards a sixth mass species extinction. And it is the widespread lack of awareness which seems a major barrier to action. Most future degradation is likely to accur in Central and South America, Sub-Saharan Africa and Asia as unprecedented growth in consumption, population and life expectancy, and advances in technology will potentially quadruple the size of the global economy in the first half of the twenty first century. The report highlights in great detail the massive impact humans are having on the planet now and in the future. Links between climate change, land degradation, biodiversity loss and agricultural practices require *simultaneous and coordinated use of diverse policy instruments* and *responses at the institutional, governance, community and individual levels*. Typically such responses are not yet happening anywhere in the world.

In 2016 another arm of the United Nations, the UN Environment Programme (UNEP) published its *Global Environmental Outlook (GEO6)*[8]; *regional assessments* listing the most severe environmental problems in different parts of the world. In Latin America and the Caribbean $CO_2$, methane and nitrous oxide emissions increased, largely as a result of increased cattle farming. Over 80% of Amazon deforestation resulted from additional cattle ranching. Extreme weather events have occurred more frequently and the Andean glaciers, source of much of the freshwater for millions of people, are shrinking. In Asia and the Pacific *increasing unsustainable consumption patterns have led to worsening air pollution, water scarcity and waste generation, threatening human and environmental health. ... Extensive agriculture, palm oil and rubber plantations, aquaculture and illegal trade in wildlife are causing environmental degradation and biodiversity loss*. This region continues to be the most disaster prone, suffering 41% of all natural disasters reported over the last 20 years. More than 1million hectares of forest is destroyed each year releasing vast quantities of $CO_2$. 30% of people in the region use drinking water contaminated by human faeces, and uncontrolled dumping is still the main waste disposal method in the region. In West Asia there is a rise in the amount of degraded land and spreading desertification. Groundwater is over-exploited whilst demand for water is increasing. Continuous conflict in the region is a major cause of severe environmental damage, which, in turn endangers human health by raising levels of pollution of air, water and soil. Climate change is expected to exacerbate water stress in this region in years to come. It is also likely to impact severely on Africa, where land degradation, air pollution (particularly from the widespread use of wood biomass for cooking), and deforestation are of concern. Over-cultivation, innefficient irrigation practices and overgrazing will lead to reduced agricultural productivity, reduced food security and increased migration. In North America the coastal environment is increasingly threatened by excessive plant nutrient pollution, ocean acidification and sea level rise. There is an increasing frequency both of droughts and of devastating floods. The Arctic region has warmed at twice the global average since 1980, leading to dramatic decline in summer sea ice. Europe is not included in this UNEP assessment, but environmental changes will be similar. I discussed in the previous chapter how excessive fertiliser use damages the environment, particularly the water environment[10], leading to the somewhat disconcerting conclusion that the costs of use outweigh the benefits of application. Manufactured fertilisers are not the sole cause. Animal manures, particularly from intensively farmed areas, also cause environmental problems, as highlighted in a WWF paper published in the 'Guardian[11], calling for a 40% reduction in cow numbers in the Netherlands because volumes of manure exceed the legal limits for spreading locally.

Is it surprising then that agriculture in the developed countries at least, feels under pressure from environmental groups, and increasingly from politicians, to change from what has become 'normal' commercial agricultural practice to something which is less damaging to the natural environment? Inevitably this creates tension between farmers and environmentalists. I began this book by suggesting that most farmers are environmentalists at heart, but they are also trying to make an economic success of their business to support themselves and their families. Economic pressures on farming restrict the options available for most commercial farmers; either they try to be as efficient as possible to make a profit despite ever increasing pressure to cut their farm gate prices, or they try to generate greater margins by exploiting 'niche' markets. A principal interest of governments is to ensure their populations are adequately supplied with safe, wholesome food at reasonable prices. In my lifetime this has meant the farmgate price of food consistently falling as a proportion of average consumer income. Increasing productivity, through increasing yields and reducing (mainly) fixed costs, (such as labour), and growing the size of the business to gain economies of scale, have been the primary means of economic survival for most farmers.

As a result, the environment has suffered. When problems started to be evident to most people in the 1980's, the UK government introduced the forerunners of today's environmental schemes. Farmers were encouraged to rein back on damaging practices on the most valuable areas for nature by the offer of compensation for income foregone. In 2018 Defra proposed '*a six point framework for sustainable farming*'[12]. This encourages the production of healthy, nutritious food whilst addressing degradation of soil and improvement of soil quality, helping wildlife recover and thrive, keeping rivers and seas free of pollution and looking after the landscape. The final proposal seeks to reduce agricultural greenhouse gas emissions and manage some of the consequences of climate change, (for instance, through deliberately allowing the flooding of agricultural land to protect downstream cities from damaging storms). These proposals, which, after consultation, will eventually translate into government policies, owe much to the commitment made in the UK Climate Change Act (2008), which requires a 5 yearly assessment of the risks to the UK of current and predicted climate change. The second risk assessment[13] in this series concentrated on the choice between protecting farmland from flooding or sea inundation compared with protecting other areas such as towns and cities. It also highlighted risks both to soil and to farm productivity that could be the result of changes in rainfall patterns and extreme weather events, including concerns over regional water abstraction rates, which could require increasing restrictions to be applied to the total water available for crop irrigation in some areas and in some years. Pressure from environmental agencies and NGO's now commands increasing Ministerial attention and this is reflected in slowly changing policy priorities. Farmers are inevitably concerned about the implications for their livelihoods. Will there be adequate compensation for income foregone in future? Will the bureaucracy in managing and auditing environmental schemes be oppressive? Will systems be developed to value fairly the 'externalities' which agriculture provides to the community? I will pick up on this in more detail later.

Before I do that, I need to broaden the scope of the debate. Commercial farming operates in a competitive environment, not simply between individual farmers within one country, but internationally. The industry in each country is invariably made up of a huge number of, usually, small and very diverse businesses. The complex interrelationship of farming with the environment and with different social structures means that the sector has developed a vast and varied web of support systems, protectionist policies and legislative measures, applied different in each country. All governments seek to feed their populations adequately, securely and, if possible, cheaply, but they also have a duty toward their own primary producers. Given the complexity and diversity of the industry and of national arrangements to support and regulate it, it is no surprise that international trade agreements on agriculture, whether bilateral or multilateral, through organisations such as the World Trade Organisation (WTO), have consistently proved elusive. Politicians and farmers regularly raise concerns over what constitutes a 'level playing field' – whether farmers in one country are more or less advantaged over those in competitor countries, or if consumers may expect imported produce of similar quality or safety standards to home produced fare. Such disputes bedevil agricultural trade negotiations between countries and trading blocs.

This book is primarily about how the world might be properly fed in years to come, without causing environmental and social armageddon. It argues that very significant changes to production systems should necessarily start now in order to achieve long term outcomes. But there is an evident disconnect between what is needed now in countries such as the UK, to achieve future goals, and the economic signals received by farmers from the current market place. After 70 years of official encouragement and relentless market pressure to increase efficiency and produce cheap food, it may take some time to convince many farmers that they should (in their perception) become 'park-keepers' instead. They will go along with well researched innovations which enable more productivity from fewer inputs, (provided, of course that the risks of economic failure are not excessively high), and most will accept additional targeted environmental measures, if these are compensated through payment of government subsidies or through better farmgate prices, and that they do not involve too much additional 'red-tape'. All of these arguments are coloured by the lack of equitable international trade agreements and the complex ways in which individual countries seek to maintain domestic food security, deal with social problems in rural areas and protect environments. And they are subject to lobbying by sectoral interest groups whose strength and political 'clout' varies from country to country.

Buckwell's argument[14] (see previous chapter), is that for developed agricultural systems such as the UK, it may be more appropriate to tip the balance in favour of environmental policies over increased production. Within Europe and North America it should not be so much of a challenge to meet future food needs even if crop and animal yield increases are slowed as a result of more environmentally sustainable technologies. This is particularly so if, as part of the overall solution to the challenges we face, we eat more healthily and sustainably. This topic demands a chapter by itself (see chapter 9). Where additional food is really needed is where populations are increasing at greater rates than in the UK and Europe, which, in general are those areas of the world where climate change is more severe, poverty is widespread, governance often poor, and farmers often face severe challenges. The application of suitably adapted basic technologies to these areas would seem an obvious priority.

The basic instincts of farmers the world over are similar. They work in and with their environment but generally their livelihood comes from what they produce to sell. Many poor farmers face the stark choice between damaging the environment and being unable to feed their families. When there is no spare money dare they take the risk of purchasing improved seeds, basic fertiliser or new technology? If their tenure on the land is not secure can they afford to consider the long term damage caused by short term exploitation? In developing countries women are responsible for 60-80% of food production, but represent between 5-30% of landholders. '*If they had the same access as men to productive resources,*' FAO estimate,[15] '*they could increase yields by 20-30% raising total agricultural output in developing countries by 2.5-4%*'. Not only does environmental damage occur in these regions through poverty and lack of government control, but through lack of knowledge, poor storage facilities, poor infrastructure, lack of effective markets and inneffective regulation and government.

So the debate in western democracies between environmentalists and farmers has much less impact when seen in the global context. There is a widely held view that food surpluses from developed economies can make up for deficiencies in developing ones. In the US, in particular, 'food aid' is widely used as a means of supporting the price of domestic agriculture by exporting surplus production. Whilst such aid is vital in extreme food crises it is effectively undercutting the ability of the recipient country to develop its own agriculture. Were that to happen in reverse, the US would undoubtedly cry 'foul' against such 'dumping' practices. For social and economic reasons it is important for nations to develop their own agriculture so long as it can be reasonably cost competitive, given 'the level playing field' I described earlier.

Development of local agricultural systems which I briefly described in the last chapter is essential to meet future food challenges, but it also needs to be balanced with proper environmental protection. In some areas it is already be too late to reclaim what has been lost. Earlier in this chapter I gave several instances where dramatic decline in biodiversity has already occurred, soils have been lost or degraded and water polluted. In some countries, such as China, government is alert to the problems and is taking, albeit very late, some mitigating action. It claims to have effectively contained desertification in the northern, north eastern and north western areas through re-afforestation. 60 years ago 8.6% of China was forested, and by 2016 this had grown to 21.66%[16]. Other governments, such as Indonesia, continue to allow massive deforestation and degradation of valuable peat forest lands. Still others have weak or venal governments either incapable of regulating environmental decline or actively conniving in short term exploitation.

Against this background it is important to explore new avenues of thinking which dare to challenge the modern form of capitalism which encourages short term strategies and drives over-exploitation of world resources without regard to longer term or hidden costs to society or the planet. A policy recommendation to the World Bank[17] *in 2015* states '*In the face of a rapidly overheating climate, collapsing fisheries, degraded soil, depleted water resources, vanishing species and other challenges directly related to agriculture, we can no longer afford to pursue a flawed accounting system*'. This theme was taken up by Bank of England Governor, Mark Carney, in a speech at Lloyds of London in 2015[18] when he brought the attention of the financial world to the 'time-horizon' mismatch, most clearly illustrated by climate related financial risk – that the long term horizon would be continually disregarded with potentially catastrophic consequences. The Banks chief economist, Andrew Haldane[19] had already indicated that recent trends toward short-termism in the financial sector had become worse in recent years.

'Natural Capital' is defined as 'the stock of renewable and non-renewable resources – water, land, air, biodiversity (animals and plants), forests, soils – that yield a flow of benefits, often termed ecosystem services'[20]. Typically, this natural capital has not been included in standard forms of accounting, largely because it was widely considered that it could be taken for granted. We now know differently. Our natural capital base is deteriorating rapidly as mankind exploits it beyond the rate of natural renewal. These so called 'externalities' cannot continue to be overlooked any longer. The UK Government, as I noted in the Foreword, is dipping its toe into the water by proposing an as yet unknown and limited scale of ecosystem service payments to UK farmers who comply with strict conditions of husbandry.

The High Level Expert Group on Sustainable Finance[ibid] recommended that the EU Commission should '*encourage and support the development and use of standards, metrics and methods for quantifying, reporting and managing natural capital risks and opportunities in decisions by financial institutions. They should also consider accounting standards ... and examine how natural capital could better be accounted for in economic valuations*'. A good deal of work on how to bring externalities into mainstream accounting practice and commercial and political decision making is now underway in many academic institutions across the world.[21]

To be meaningful in terms of a widely used and useful accounting system which, if universally adopted, would effectively change current economic practice to a longer term horizon, a wide range of externalities would need to be assessed. Each crop, agricultural system and supply chain would have its own particular set of environmental impacts, both positive and negative. Some of these may be economically 'visible', but others may not. How can evaluations of impact be consistent and comparable both within and between different systems? Whilst some risks can be evaluated in monetary terms, others may need to be addressed qualitatively, as for instance ethical considerations, such as animal welfare, or social implications, such as the extent to which a particular system helps address local food insecurity. Within the UNEP sponsored TEEB[22] (*'The Economics of Ecosystems and Biodiversity Project'*), the concept of a framework matrix for enabling decision making is suggested, which would need to be context specific and depend on the application being considered. For instance, in terms of business analysis, the matrix of Product A could be compared with that of

Product B, whilst for policy evaluation Policy scenario A could be compared with Policy scenario B. Clearly different methods of valuation may apply. It will also be evident that data on which to base sensible valuations, where these are appropriate, may not be readily available. Developing such data sets will be a vital early step in seeking to mainstream this new form of accounting, which in turn is crucial in stimulating changed attitudes to what constitutes human progress. In many areas of the world poor or venal governance pays little heed to environmental damage in the pursuit of short term gain. It is surely incumbent on developed economies to create and use economic systems which encourage a long term view in order to persuade and encourage the others to emulate them? I will return in a later chapter to the difficulties this is likely to face.

In the short term, farmers, in developed countries at least, will need to change the way they farm to embrace the concept of natural capital and other issues which have not yet been effectively addressed by government or the 'market'. To what extent they will be compensated by public funding remains to be seen. Payment for provision of public access to farmland, or for growing crops to sustain wild bird populations will be easier for the tax payer to accept. It may be harder to achieve compensation from the public purse for less easily measured benefits such as carbon sequestration in soils. Farmers will hope that the 'market' will recognise, and will be prepared to pay more for instance, for the additional costs which arise from free range as opposed to 'intensive' animal production methods, or lower yielding crops grown with reduced fertiliser or spray. This happens with most organic products, but once 'niche' production becomes 'mainstream' any price premium generally disappears. Suggestions that all consumers are willing to pay more for 'better' food are often made but rarely borne out in practice. Farmers are price takers rather than price makers, and in reaction to pressures to change the way they farm many will claim that their businesses cannot be 'green' unless their accounts are in the 'black'.

Farmers in developing countries with low standards of education, limited budgetary resources and poor government leadership will find it challenging to provide a better environment. Improved technology to raise production without increasing farmed area will help, but that alone will not address the wider problems of increasing exploitation to meet increasing demand for food. We need to look at means by which the demand curve can be lowered, through changing consumption patterns and reducing food waste. The next chapter considers waste reduction.

# Chapter 8

# Waste

'There is no Planet B'.

*Emmanuel Macron (speech to US Congress, April 2018)*

In preparation for a presentation to a conference on challenges facing future food systems a colleague of mine recently conducted an informal survey of university students and young farmers on what they would prioritise for action. Almost everyone selected a reduction of food waste as their first choice. Perhaps that is not surprising. In an affluent 'throw-away' society such as the UK most of us recognise how cheap and plentiful food has become, and how that bounty encourages both waste and over consumption. The media is full of stories about diet and health alongside concerns over 'wonky' fruit and vegetables being discarded by supermarkets, oversize portions of food in restaurants and the usefulness or otherwise of 'sell-by dates' on packaging. Whilst most people are aware of these issues, few know that waste food accounts for 8% of global greenhouse gas emissions – everything from the $CO_2$ emitted in production of fertiliser to grow the crop to the methane given off as the food rots. This amount of food requires an area bigger than the whole of China on which to grow every year. Such profligacy comes at very considerable economic and environmental cost.

Compared with other challenges we have discussed so far, reducing food waste appears to be the 'low hanging fruit', the easiest problem to address. According to WRAP (Waste and Resources Action Programme), a UK Charity that works with governments, businesses, local authorities and consumers to reduce waste, the average UK household in 2015 threw away £470 of edible food, amounting to 7.3million tonnes of waste with a retail value of £13billion. Of that total 4.4m.tonnes was 'avoidable' waste that was edible at some point before being binned, such as mouldy bread or out-of-date packaged food. The rest consisted of scraps such as egg shells, tea bags and potato peelings[1].

There are some indications that there has been a recent decline in the good progress made by industry in tackling waste in the supply chain since WRAP began its work in 2007. To remedy this the 2015 Report announced the 'Courtauld Commitment 2025', which aims to reduce food waste in the UK food chain by 20% on a per person basis by 2025. It will do this through better consumer information and advice, common guidelines on storage instructions, date labelling and portion size control, government incentives and regulations. Business strategies to minimise waste need to be more transparent and cooperative.

As an illustration of some of the difficulties in achieving real reductions in food waste Swiss researchers analysed the quantity and quality of food losses in the Swiss potato supply chain from field to fork[2]. Across the entire potato value chain approximately 53-55% of the fresh potato harvest, and 41-46% of processing potatoes were lost. Half the loss occurred because potatoes did not meet exacting quality standards. Interestingly, losses in organic supply chains were higher than non-organic because they failed more often to satisfy the high quality standards demanded. Supermarkets have driven up quality standards to a point where a significant proportion of vegetable products in particular are discarded in the field or during processing and packaging. A number of UK multiple retailers recently began to offer a range of 'non-standard' vegetables at reduced prices to try to counter criticism of 'enforced wastage' lower down the chain, and with clever marketing, such as labelling 'wonky fruit' at reduced prices, some consumers are becoming less 'picky' in their buying choices.

Of course food waste occurs at all levels of the supply chain, but where this wastage actually occurs varies between developed and developing countries. In general, most wastage in developing countries is pre and post harvest loss, due to basic agricultural inefficiencies and technological and infrastructure limitations, such as poor storage or lack of good roads or transport to market. In high income countries such as the UK most waste occurs after leaving the farm. Nearly three quarters of this is avoidable waste, thrown away by consumers. Most of the remainder is lost during manufacture, but much of that is not fit for human consumption. The distribution and retail sector surprisingly wastes an average of only 3%[3]. The products most prone to household waste are those with a short shelf-life (perishables). Consumers often over-purchase these products and more is wasted through lack of adequate cooking skills, poor storage facilities and lack of time to utilise 'left-overs'.

Many things can be done to tackle food waste. They include breeding programmes and genetic research to improve disease resistance and storage life. While these take time to work through, in the short term growers can improve growing and harvesting techniques to minimise damage and loss. Storage, transport, grading and packaging systems can all be improved. Beyond the farm gate shelf life can be improved with preservatives or through product reformulation. Innovative solutions include new sensing technologies and microbiological control inside 'smart' packaging. Recent pressure to reduce or remove plastic packaging for environmental reasons may have the paradoxical effect of slowing progress in reducing food waste.

Persuading consumers to change their eating habits or to accept products which taste or look different is never easy. How to influence consumer choice is the subject of a book in itself. In the UK, it appears that people who do save money by wasting less food then spend about half that saving to 'trade-up' to more premium grocery products[4]. Government has an important role in providing guidance, regulation and financial incentives to encourage good retail practice. It can support use of better packaging materials, require effective and helpful product labelling and provide education and training to industry and consumers. But it can also be regarded negatively by many as a 'nanny state', usurping consumers freedom of choice. Much academic debate has taken place over the extent to which consumers can be 'nudged' toward appropriate choices, rather than 'bullied'. Given this context it is likely that any change will be gradual and, even if policies remain consistent, they may take a generation to work through.

Consistency and clarity of policy is dependant on clear objectives, sound science and general agreement of the end point. As we shall see in the next chapter researchers have so far shown too little consistency or agreement over many issues involving dietary change. That makes it even more difficult to achieve cultural consumer change in this area anytime soon. Whether the somewhat simpler objective of reducing food wastage at the consumer level can be achieved more quickly remains to be seen, although one academic study suggests that if over-eating, (defined as food consumption in excess of nutritional requirements), is also considered a waste, this would imply almost 50% of all food production globally is wasted[5]. In these terms the scale of the problem is immense, and deserving of urgent and serious attention by governments worldwide to help ensure our food supply is sustainable.

In December 2017 the Economist Intelligence Unit launched its *Food Sustainability Index 2017*, which graded the performance of 34 countries in reducing food waste, supporting environmentally friendly agriculture and encouraging healthy nutrition[6]. France topped the list, having been the first country to introduce specific food waste legislation, requiring supermarkets to donate food approaching its sell by date to charities or food banks, together with other measures to reduce food wastage in schools, and prompting companies to include relevant data in their social and environmental reports. Annual food waste per head in France is 106kg, less than a third of that in Australia and around 10% that of the worst performing country, United Arab Emirates, which, as well as having the highest income per head of the 34 countries, threw away almost 1000kg of food per person per year.

In America the National Resources Defence Council (NRDC) is roughly equivalent to WRAP in the UK. It works to make America's food system more efficient and less wasteful. In 2017 it published a Report entitled '*How America is losing up to 40% of its food from Farm to Fork to Landfill*'[7]. Making a difference to food wastage in America presents an enormous challenge in a nation which prizes individual freedom of choice and 'small' government. In a global context the average American consumer wastes 10 times as much as as someone living in South East Asia or Sub-Saharan Africa. That wasted food accounts for 25% of US freshwater consumption and the use of huge amounts of chemicals, energy and land. When tipped into landfills the waste food produces almost 25% of US methane emissions.

US household food waste accounts for 43% (2015) of total food waste, whilst farms account for 16%. Compare this with China where more food is lost through poor storage and transportation than at the retail or consumption levels[8]. Or with India, where, because of lack of adequate post harvest and food processing infrastructure, more than 20% of cereals and up to 40% of vegetables and fruits go to waste before getting anywhere near consumers[9].

The fact that more than I billion tonnes of food worldwide never makes it to the table, when nearly 800m people – 1 in 9 globally – are undernourished is both a tragedy and an indictment of the world we live in. In Mozambique, where smallholder farmers store crops in sacks as their main form of saving, 61% reported significant damage to the grain through pest contamination[10]. To help reduce these losses ways need to be found to improve storage methods, perhaps with something as simple as improved triple layer plastic storage bags which can be hermetically sealed. Since 2007 the Gates Foundation, through the US government *Feed the Future* initiative, have distributed these bags to over 33,000 villages in Sub-Saharan Africa and Asia, helping to reduce post-harvest loss for farmers by 40%[11]. Lack of power supply, refrigeration and effective cold chain transport systems condemns many areas across the developing world to a high wastage rate for many foodstuffs. The Global Food Security Report states, '*There is little point in greater agricultural productivity unless infrastructure can deliver food to the consumer*'[12]. The Nigerian Minister of Agriculture, Akinwumi Adesina confirmed this view[13] in an article in the Wall Street Journal. Addressing the youth unemployment problem in rural areas of Africa, he argued for investment in rural infrastructure, better communications, extra warehousing capacity and siting of food processing facilities in the countryside, to revive flagging economies, offer employment opportunities and reduce waste.

While it is clear that measures to address food waste are country specific it is also evident that they present a global challenge demanding international cooperation and understanding. Over the last decade the international community has recognised the importance of the topic and begun to take action. The first step was to set food loss and waste reduction goals. Target number 12.3 of the UN Sustainable Development Goals (SDG's), adopted in September 2015, calls for halving global food waste at retail and consumer levels by 2030, and for significantly reducing all other areas of food loss. In addition to these targets the Committee of World Food Security has called on '*all public, private and civil society actors to promote a common understanding of food loss and waste, and to create an enabling environment for its 'food-use-not-waste' agenda, especially for monitoring, measuring and reporting targets*'[14]. One outcome of this appeal was an announcement at the World Economic Forum in Davos, (January 2016), of the formation of a 'Champions 12.3' coalition of 30 food industry leaders committed to mobilize action to reduce food loss and waste globally. Chair of the group is Dave Lewis, Group CEO of Tesco plc, with other members drawn from major food companies, government ministers, research institutions, farmer organisations and civil society groups.

At the same Davos gathering the Rockefeller Foundation announced its '*Yieldwise*' initiative[16] with $130m funding, initially focussing on reducing losses on fruit, vegetables and staple crops in Kenya, Nigeria and Tanzania, where up to half all food grown is lost. This and other initiatives sit alongside the United Nations Environment Programme's (UNEP) '*Think, Eat,*

*Save'* initiative[17] in partnership with FAO, to raise awareness of and promote practices and policies to reduce food loss and waste.

As I noted at the head of chapter 7, *'we cannot manage what we do not measure'*. There is a lack of consensus on what defines food loss and waste, and many countries have deficient or rudimentary data systems to measure what is going on in the various parts of the food chain. At the G20 Agriculture Ministers meeting in Turkey in 2015, IFPRI and FAO launched the *'Technical Platform on Food Loss and Waste[18]'* in an attempt to standardise data collection around the world, and this was followed in 2016 by the *'Food Loss and Waste Protocol's Accounting and Reporting Standard[19]'* produced in partnership by the World Resources Institute (WRI), UNEP, FAO and WRAP.

With these building blocks in place the target of 50% reduction in global retail and consumer food waste by 2050 may be achievable. Progress in reducing waste on farm and post-harvest will depend on technological developments in richer countries and investment in infrastructure, storage, better marketing and education in developing nations (particularly of women farmers, who carry out the majority of the farm work). Seeking further reduction in global food waste, though, requires significant change in consumer perceptions and habits. This suggests a 'generational' change, probably in parallel with dietary change, so it is to this subject that I turn in the next chapter.

# Chapter 9

# Diet and Health

'To lengthen thy life, lessen thy meals'.

*Ben. Franklin (Poor Roger's Almanac, 1733)*

*The Big Mac index* has been published annually by 'The Economist' since 1986, and is regarded as a simplified indicator of the purchasing power of an economy over time. It is shown as the price in US dollars for a Big Mac, country by country. However, if Big Macs are taken as representative of 'fast food' prices in general, the index also indicates the relative price change of these items compared with so called 'healthy foods' such as fruit and vegetables. It is clear that in most economies for which data exists, the Big Mac has become cheaper relative to these other foods since the early 1990's, and especially when compared with the prices for fruit and vegetables.

Data from the World Health Organisation (WHO 2015-17)[1] child obesity surveillance initiative shows that southern Europe, the birthplace of the Mediterranean diet, now has the fattest children in Europe. And evidence from the Institute for Development Studies[2] and Oxfam shows that the sudden rise in the price of basic foods following the 2007 financial crisis caused millions across the developing world to switch to cheaper 'junk food' alternatives, high in sugars, fats and salt. People who move to urban areas, where they can earn more also have less time to grow and prepare their own food. They too come to rely more on westernised 'fast food' which is known to be addictive.

A study published in *The Lancet Global Health* in 2015[3], the largest study of its kind covering 4.5bn adults, found that on average older adults consume better diets than younger adults, and women better diets than men. Unhealthy eating habits are outpacing healthy eating habits across most regions of the world. A generational change in dietary habits is occurring very widely, but it is heading in the wrong direction. In consequence many health professionals are now asking whether the direction of travel can be reversed and if so, what actions are needed, and over what time scale?

Trying to change eating habits is a complex business. As a report from the Overseas Development Institute[4] (odi) states *'In general, there is little appetite amongst politicians or the public in high income countries to take strong measures to influence future diets. Politicians are fearful of meddling with diets, and alienating farming and food-industry interests. It seems that this reflects public opinion, with many people seeing food choices as a matter of personal freedom. Most people hate the prospect of regulation of their favoured foods; they see taxation of unhealthy foods and ingredients as unfair, and aquiesce, often only lukewarmly, in response to public information and education campaigns. Couple this with lobbying from food industries, and the political will to affect diet withers'*.

This rather bleak conclusion appears to be borne out in the reaction of the US Government to the publication of its 2015 US Dietary Guidelines Report[5]. In summary, the committee found that *'Meeting current and future food needs will depend on two concurrent approaches: altering individual dietary choices and patterns, and developing agricultural and production practices that reduce environmental impacts and conserve resources, while still meeting food and nutrition needs.'* There was heavy pressure on the US government from vested interests in the food industry to reduce the impact of this document and effectively negate the section on dietary change and sustainability. Yet the accumulating mass of evidence of damage done to human health and the environment by modern food consumption patterns together with the rising power of animal welfare groups arguing for lower meat consumption, has stimulated some countries to take political action, albeit limited and often uncoordinated.

In 2013 Mexico, which has one of the most obese and sugar-addicted populations in the world, imposed a 10% tax on sugary drinks. The tax appears to have had some success in cutting consumption. The UK followed suit in 2017 with a multi-tiered tax based on the actual sugar levels in high-sugar drinks, joining around 30 countries where such a tax has already been introduced or is planned. Such taxes don't always succeed. Efforts to levy a soda tax in Chicago foundered after two months[6], following a similar failure in Santa Fe a few months earlier. The soda companies resistant to the tax, paid for advertising, lobbyists and political contributions to build a case which proved too strong for the city authorities to fight and win. Coca Cola, the world's largest brand by value and sales spent $4bn on worldwide advertising on its products in 2015, which was equivalent to the World Health Organisation's entire 2 year 2014/5 budget. The food industry as a whole spent about $40bn on advertising. For every $1spent by WHO in trying to reduce consumption of disease inducing Western style diets, more than $500 was spent by the food industry promoting them[7].

The WHO[8] advocates taxes on unhealthy foods and subsidies on healthy ones, citing *'reasonable and increasing evidence that appropriately designed taxes on sugar sweetened beverages would result in proportional reductions in consumption, especially if aimed at raising the retail price by 20% or more'*. There is similar strong evidence that subsidies for fresh fruit and vegetables that reduce prices by 10-30% are effective in increasing fruit and vegetable consumption. *'Greater effects on net energy intake and weight may be accomplished by combining subsidies on fruit and vegetables and taxation of target foods and beverages.'* Moves by some UK supermarkets to reduce food waste by selling mis-shapen produce at reduced prices could have the twin effect of increasing consumption of healthy foods.

In the introduction to *Sustainable Diets*, a book by Pamela Mason and Tim Lang[9], the authors comment that they wrote the book firstly because the subject of food is not high enough on the political agenda, and secondly, to counter the tendency to devote more attention to production than to consumption. Mason and Lang refer to the *'mass psychology of diet'* whereby strong marketing and exploitation of changing social norms have transformed the eating experience from a *'need'* to a *'want'*, (at least in wealthier countries), in an environment where there is almost too much food, rather than too little. Competition for a bigger share of the consumers purse leads to constant innovation within the food industry, and associated pressure to add value by further processing, and to increase volume sales by whatever means are permissable.

As the WHO statement indicates, dietary changes which are good for human health and for the environment are much more wide ranging than the current concentration of political intervention on sugary drinks would imply. There is now widespread and strong evidence of the association between unhealthy diets, excessive food consumption and rising levels of a range of non-communicable diseases (NCD's). *The Global Burden of Disease study[10]*, conducted over 25 years in 195 countries, collected data on cause of death, disease and injury since 1980. While deaths from infectious diseases fell sharply, those related to lifestyle choices soared. These included heart disease, stroke, cancer and diabetes. In particular, the analysis showed the incidence of obesity between 1980 and 2015 had doubled in more than 70 countries, and continuously increased in most other countries. The rate of increase in childhood obesity in many countries was greater than that in adults.

Bad diets and unhealthy lifestyles are believed to contribute to 7 in 10 deaths worldwide and to a significant proportion of poor health or disability. High blood pressure, fuelled by obesity and lack of exercise tops the list of risk factors, followed by smoking, high blood sugar and high Body Mass Index (BMI). Discussing the study results the authors express grave concern over the prevalence of people carrying excess body weight, including high BMI and obesity. Taking all the listed causes of death together they accounted for about 4 million deaths and 120 million 'disability-adjusted-life -years' worldwide in 2015. 70% of deaths related to high BMI were due to cardiovascular disease, and more than 60% of those deaths occurred among obese persons. (WHO define a BMI of more than 25 as overweight, and abnormal or excessive fat accumulation resulting in a BMI of more than 30 as obese.)

The authors go on to state '... *the prevalence of obesity has increased over recent decades, which indicates that the problem is not simply a function of income or wealth. Changes in the food environment and food systems are probably major drivers. Increased availability, accessibility, and affordability of energy dense foods, along with intense marketing of such foods could explain excess energy intake and weight gain among different populations. The reduced opportunities for physical activity that have followed urbanisation and other changes in the built environment have also been considered as potential drivers; however, these changes generally preceded the global increase in obesity and are less likely to be major contributors.*'

This view gains support from a Foresight report commissioned in 2016 by the Gates Foundation and UK DfID[11]. Taking a global view, it concludes that food systems are failing us. '*Those who would benefit from consuming more animal source foods, fruit, vegetables and pulses often find them unafford-able*' ... '*Today's food systems are too focused on food quantity and not food quality. They are not helping consumers to make healthy and affordable food choices consistent with optimal nutrition outcomes. In fact the trend is in the opposite direction*'. In the preface to the report the message to policy makers is stark: Unless they '*act decisively to control overweight, obesity and diet related disease and accelerate efforts to reduce undernutrition, all countries will pay a heavy price in terms of mortality, physical health, mental well being, economic losses and degradation of the environment.'*

So what can policy makers do to change relatively recently acquired eating habits, and to persuade producers, processors and retailers, (together representing the whole food industry), to take greater account of health concerns? It is not a simple problem to which there are clear and straight-forward answers. Although the basic building blocks of a healthy diet are widely known and accepted, there is widespread confusion amongst consumers when it comes to choosing specific items, as exemplified by an American survey[12] where almost 80% of respondents reported receiving conflicting advice about what they should or should not eat. Although scientific studies were generally considered more trustworthy than other sources, the reporting of these by general media often failed to provide context or tell the whole story. Widespread claims by manufacturers or by single issue pressure groups, such as vegans or anti-GMO groups, only served to sow more confusion. In trying to cover all the bases the Food and Agriculture Organisations' (FAO) definition of a 'sustainable diet'[13] includes not only consideration of nutrition and health but also protection of biodiversity, optimisation of natural and human resources, affordability, availability and cultural relevance.

It is widely accepted that a sustainable diet should be mainly plant based with some meat and dairy with minimal levels of sugar and fat, but there is considerable divergence of opinion, even among experts, as to what consti-tutes a 'good plate' for different individuals and for different cultures. In many areas of the world there is a paucity of data on which to base recommendations, particularly in the less developed countries. Even in wealthy countries with good data sources, there are difficulties linking different databases. We need a guide, as recommended by Mason and Lang[14] which will enable policymakers to give the public a clear indication of the constituents of a healthy diet taking account of the extra layers of complexity within the FAO definition. This would need to address not only the possible constituents of sustainable diets, but also the problem of over-consumption. Much of the current obesity epidemic can be blamed on human greed and ignorance. Sugar rich foods and high calorie processed foods are habit forming and can cause problems if consumed in excess of bodily requirements. Food outlets often compete for customers by offering bigger portions. Domestic consumers are attracted by buy-one-get-one-free (BOGOF) offers in supermarkets. Sweets and sugary drinks are positioned at children's eye level at store checkouts, to encourage that extra, unplanned purchase.

Reducing the amount of meat we eat is a hot topic in developed economies. The British Dietetic Association advocates a reduction in red and processed meat in the UK diet, to be replaced by appropriate plant based proteins such as beans and pulses[15]. Cardiovascular disease and colorectal cancer are increasingly linked to red and processed meat consumption, and several other types of cancer are associated with high BMI. Along with high sugar intake, high saturated fat is linked to the explosion in incidence of type 2 diabetes. Having raised animals for meat all my working life I am very familiar with expounding the benefits of meat as a source of essential protein and micronutrients such as vitamins A and B12, calcium, iron and zinc. But international nutritional guidelines suggest a goal of 80-90g of meat per person per day with 50g of that coming from red meat. People living in higher income countries consume, on average 200-250g meat per person per day. At the same time over 800 million people globally receive less than the guideline amount and are malnourished[16]. Lack of equitable distribution leads to problems of both over and under nutrition and to very different health and economic problems which I touched on in chapter 6.

The reason for arguing for a reduction in the average consumption of meat globally is wider than the implications for health. In chapter 6, (on research and technology in agriculture), I outlined growing concern about antibiotic use in animal production adding to the risk of the development of bacterial resistance in human medicine. And in chapters 1 (population) and 4 (water) I noted the increasing global demand for meat based diets together with the concomitant increase in global use of land, water and other resources that this implies. Today there are about 1.5bn cattle on the planet, 1.2bn pigs and 1bn sheep[17], plus a huge and fast growing chicken industry. In 1960 global production of all meats totalled about 45m tonnes. Today that figure is 263m tonnes and this is projected to rise to 445m tonnes by 2050, a tenfold rise within less than 100 years. For the first time ever, in 2016, a third of all grain produced globally was fed to livestock. Ruminant livestock use 70% of all agricultural land, about one third of all land on the planet. Admittedly much of this land is unsuitable for growing crops but particularly in Latin America the conversion of much of the 2.7m hectares of tropical forest to pasture each year is due to expansion of cattle ranching and of soya bean production for intensive animal feed. Meat production also demands a great deal of water. About 15,000 litres of water are needed to produce 1kg of beef compared to 1600 litres to grow 1kg of wheat.

Stock farming is by far the largest contributor of greenhouse gases from the food and agriculture sector and produces about 14.5% of all human induced emissions from all sources. Beef and milk production account for the largest proportion of this, mainly through production of enteric methane in the digestion process. There are very considerable differences in environmental impacts which are related to efficiency of production, high-lighting the importance of developing technical improvements in animal breeding and feeding. Although important for increasing supplies and keeping down consumer prices, intensive production (especially of white meats such as chicken or pork) has many critics who argue that such systems are unnatural or cruel. Their influence, together with increasing health warnings about over-consumption of red and processed meat in particular, appears to be having some effect on recent consumption trends in the EU, as illustrated by a 2017 survey of consumer expectations by the Dutch bank ING[18]. Meat consumption in western and southern Europe is falling from a high level, with consumers indicating further reduction in future. Some Governments appear keen to support measures to encourage this change. According to The Farm Animal Investment Risk and Return (FAIRR) network[19] some signatories to the Paris climate Accord are consid-ering the imposition of 'livestock levies' – effectively taxes on meat – to discourage excessive consumption whilst also contributing to the achieve-ment of their national targets for GHG reduction to combat climate change. While some researchers are developing technologies to reduce methane emissions through modifying ruminant diets others are racing to develop 'cultured' meat, such as Quorn (made from fungal mycoprotein)[20] and other forms of non-meat substitutes

So pressure to reduce meat consumption and the search for alter-natives stems as much from those concerned about climate change as from the health lobby. A number of studies[21,22] modelling future meat consumption trends conclude that what is termed the 'business as usual' or current trend scenario would by itself cause global GHG emissions to exceed the 2°C threshold agreed at the Paris talks. Dairy has more than double the emissions impact of poultry or pork, and global consumption of dairy products continues to rise. China, for instance is predicted on current trends to increase demand more than threefold between

2010-2050 with very significant implications for emissions and land and water use[23]. The UK Committee on Climate Change[24] calls for reduction in beef, lamb and dairy production and consumption in the UK of at least 20% by 2050. Many other countries would need to emulate this to achieve global GHG emission targets.

These arguments are made from the perspective of rich countries where food is plentiful and generally affordable. But we live in a world where almost 1bn people are undernourished and a further 2bn exposed to food shortages, and where maternal malnutrition contributes to the death of around 800,000 infants each year, and child under-nutrition contributes to nearly half of all deaths of children under five globally. For these people the nutritional value of even minimal portions of meat or dairy product can be literally life-saving. Rising carbon dioxide levels in the atmosphere may reduce the levels of protein, iron and zinc in staple food crops such as rice, wheat and peas, making the situation even worse for those attempting to survive on protein deficient diets[25]. Although rice and wheat are not high in protein almost three quarters of the world population uses these two crops as their primary sources of this vital nutrient. For about 150m people in parts of Africa and Asia the loss of 5% of their dietary protein could make their diet protein deficient. In such circumstances there is no case for them to reduce meat intake. Instead the priority is how to improve animal productivity in these areas, and what needs to be done to ensure everyone has access to sufficient protein.

Ending malnutrition in all its forms and promoting sustainable agriculture by 2030, is enshrined in the second of 17 UN Sustainable Development Goals[26], which were agreed internationally in 2015. Progress made in each country is regularly monitored, and the results published. Since 2000, some progress has been made in reducing the numbers of children stunted by food shortage or malnutrition. Most progress is seen in Southern Asia, followed by Sub-Saharan Africa. The 2017 report, however, notes the reduction in foreign aid committed to agriculture by developed countries since the late 1990's and the need for enhanced investment by governments and private industry to improve agricultural productivity and to preserve indigenous genetic diversity of crop and animal species. The Consultative Group on International Agricultural Research (CGIAR) has a major role in transforming agri-food systems, and has developed a research portfolio which focuses less on staple crop breeding and more on nutrient dense crops such as legumes, which until now have been the 'poor relations' within the crop breeding industry. The intention is to improve diets locally according to need, and to improve resilience to climatic change and to price volatility by stabilising yields through greater diversity of crop types and genetics.

Plant breeding can be used to increase the micronutrient content of crops, but in the short term, for countries where micronutrient deficiencies are common, food fortification can be an option. Milk, for instance, can be fortified with vitamin D, salt with iodine, wheat flour with iron, folic acid and thiamine. Remedies can be tailored to specific needs.

An increasing number of countries are suffering the 'triple burden' of under-nutrition, micronutrient deficiencies and overnutrition, all at the same time, but within different sectors of the population. A study in East and Southern Africa by United Nations University[27] indicated a range of problems this food transition phase presents to governments. Early economic development in most countries is associated with movement of people from rural to urban areas and to lifestyles which are more sedentary. City dwellers are often wealthier but 'time-poor', encouraging increased consumption of processed and 'fast' foods, meat and dairy products, which in turn leads to the problems of obesity already discussed. Domestic supply chains often cannot produce what is required or compete on price or convenience, creating economic stress in the rural economy. Because of increasing outflow of hard currency to pay for imported food, governments often have insufficient funds to assist these hard pressed rural areas.

All of this complexity is, perhaps, best summarised by quoting from the Executive summary of the Foresight report, '*Food Systems and Diets: Facing the challenge of the 21st century)*[28]. '*Around the world, coordinated action needs to be accompanied by fundamental shifts in our understanding and in our policy actions. Much more emphasis must be given to positioning agricultural growth as a way to improve diet quality, rather than merely delivering sufficient calories. Food systems need to be repositioned from just supplying food to providing high quality diets for all. This will require policy initiatives far beyond agriculture to encompass trade, the environment and health, which harness the power of the private sector and empower consumers to demand better diets.'*

Putting on my 'farmers hat' and wondering what I should make of all of this in planning my activities and investments, were I still running my own farming business, it is clear that I would be looking at a very uncertain future. Already there are strong signals that environmental concerns will narrow the options for using many of the technical developments of the last half century, such as the genetic modification of crop varieties or more widespread use of agrochemicals . Increasing variability and extremes of weather will exacerbate the risks of crop failure or disease and probably lead to greater price volatility on world markets. The implications of bringing considerations of diet and health into agricultural and food policy, particularly for meat and dairy producers, are potentially very significant. If global challenges are to be properly addressed through greater international understanding and cooperation this implies a significant change from the current position of 'competitive protectionism'. Unwinding current support measures such as grants or subsidies is likely to be an uncomfortable experience for many farm businesses. The direction of travel, and hence the type of investment decisions I should be making, is clouded by enormous uncertainty.

For small farmers in developing countries the outlook is similarly opaque. Climatic variability is likely to be of much greater consequence than in temperate and wealthier regions. Technology may enable currently poor productivity to be improved, but access to education, capital, land security and properly functioning markets and supply chains will be vital to take advantage of these improvements. The extent to which food consumption trends change will have enormous and unforseen repercussions on individual rural economies. Farming is a long term business. To thrive it needs clarity and consistency in government policy and in the market signals it receives. Whether such clarity will emerge from the ongoing debates around food, farming, the environment and health remains to be seen. In part 2 I examine this issue further.

**Part 2**

# How to change?

# Chapter 10

# Farmers

To every complex problem there is an answer that is clear, simple and wrong'.

*H.L.Mencken*

It should be clear to readers by now that what appeared to be a straightforward, if difficult challenge, to feed future generations, is not one that lends itself to simple answers or grand overall solutions. The complexity of inter-related problems, the multitude of different challenges, including the largely unknown effects of climatic changes in different parts of the world, make this something which must be tackled with urgency and with a high level of cooperation within and between nations. I turn to the wider political and social problems in later chapters, but first it is timely to examine how the 570m farmers worldwide[1] may view the current and future challenges they face.

In the course of this book being written the UK Government was in negotiation with the EU to leave the European Union ('Brexit') in accordance with the wishes of the electorate in a referendum in 2016. Many farmers voted to leave, citing concerns such as the perceived high level of bureaucracy within the Common Agricultural Policy (CAP), their lack of influence over domestic agricultural policies, and a general disillusionment with a system which consistently failed to deliver adequate farm incomes in recent years. Others, who voted to 'remain', expressed concern at the potential loss of EU market access, the uncertainty inherent in entering a 'free trade' environment outside the EU and worries over lack of seasonal workers if EU migrant labour became unavailable. As negotiations dragged on, with no clarity of outcome, the main concern became how to plan for business with so much uncertainty surrounding future policy arrangements. Change of any kind is disruptive. Farming is a long-term operation – to raise a beef animal from conception to slaughter, for instance, may take

3 to 4 years. Without some reasonable certainty of a profitable market at the end of this process it is difficult for a small business to justify the initial investment.

Farmers are used to dealing with the uncertainties of weather, although increasing climatic variability everywhere makes life even more difficult. Adding political and regulatory uncertainty can turn an already difficult business into a precarious one. During the 1990's I was closely involved in trying to mitigate the damage done to the UK pig industry by the Government passing unilateral legislation to ban the use of sow stalls, which enabled greater productivity at less cost than more traditional systems of husbandry. At that time our main competitors in Europe faced no such restriction, giving them competitive advantage to exploit the UK market. As a result, over the following decade, almost half of all British pig farmers went out of business.

Under WTO rules, the concerns expressed by some countries about animal welfare are largely regarded as 'protectionist'. Some import restrictions on plant and animal products, claimed by some countries to reduce the risk of transfer of animal or plant diseases or to maintain the safety of domestic consumers are similarly not recognised by the rules. Trade policy is highly politicised and there is no doubt that hygiene, food safety or welfare rules are sometimes used to deny importation of goods which might threaten vested interests in the host country. There are many instances, however, when such restrictions on trade are reasonable and appropriate. I think back to the disastrous outbreak of foot and mouth disease in the UK in 2001, which cost billions of pounds to eradicate, destroyed millions of animals and caused untold misery to many livestock farmers whose livelihoods were affected. The original source of the disease was never found, but was most likely carried on illegally imported product.

As I discussed in chapter 7, there is pressure to shift agricultural support funding away from production and toward environmental goals. Farmers are naturally concerned to preserve an equitable balance between profitable business and potential environmental gain. UK and European farmers fear the balance is tipping more toward environmental interests. For example, in environmental aspects of the post 2020 Common Agricultural Policy (CAP) the European Parliament (EP) granted the Environment Committee 'shared competence' with the Agriculture Committee[2]. Furthermore the EP has regularly demonstrated its disregard for scientific evidence in banning of the use of technologies such as GMO's and, more controversially still, of the gene editing technique CRISPR-cas9 (see also chapter 6), despite these technologies being widely used around the world with no reported health or safety concerns.

In America farmers are concerned that regulation and political inconsistency threatens their livelihoods. In California, for instance, the State mandated in 2016 a reduction in methane emissions from livestock of 40% by 2030. Other States have not yet followed suit, thereby potentially disadvantaging Californian dairy farmers. Of more immediate concern to the competitiveness of Californian farmers within their own country is a unilateral requirement for migrant labourers within the State to receive a considerably enhanced minimum wage[3]. More recently Mid West farmers were caught up in trade wars initiated by President Donald Trump. In imposing penal tariffs on imports of steel and other goods from China, the Chinese responded by penalising US exports of soya bean to them, knowing that this would target the heartland of Trump supporting voters. Sadly, agriculture is all too often caught up in this kind of 'horse trading'. The provision of adequate and reasonably priced food is a fundamental duty of government, which also has overall responsibility for care of the environment and for maintaining the social fabric of the countryside. It is almost inevitable that politicians 'interfere' more with this industry than with almost any other.

Such 'interference' is not often wholly successful. According to euractiv.com [4] *'Every year 10.8million farmers working on 174m ha of agricultural land receive around €60bn of EU funding. These payments are designed to support an environmentally responsible and sustainable agricultural policy that complements the UN Sustainable Development Goals while guaranteeing Europe's food security, ... without undermining the resources or sustainable farming practices of third countries. Yet the reality is that biodiversity loss is accelerating, nitrate pollution in groundwater is rising and soil quality is being eroded'.* Around the same time that this was written the consulting firm, Andersons, compiled a report for the Prince's Countryside Fund[5] in the UK, which noted that half of all farmers surveyed were no longer making a living from farming itself, while 20% were making a loss even before accounting for family labour. This slump in incomes, (particularly severe amongst livestock farmers in 2015) affected the wider community servicing farmers, according to the chairman of the fund, Lord Curry: *'Decreased cashflow is affecting the industry as a whole, from vets to feed and machinery suppliers, to auction marts[6].'*

Compared to many other industries almost all farms are small businesses. With little control whether the market for their product is over or under supplied, their natural reaction to falling prices is to try to raise output in order to compensate for lost income, sometimes resulting in further price reductions. In many countries farmers try to work together to try to manage markets better, but everywhere the effect of increasingly variable weather conditions exacerbates the inherent volatility of farm incomes, and this is especially severe in poorer countries where governments are unable to fund measures to support low farm incomes or to mitigate the wilder fluctuations in market prices.

A 2016 UK House of Lords report[7] concluded that a degree of price volatility was essential to give proper market signals, and that moderate volatility could be managed with a variety of intervention tools by Government, and through greater proactivity by farmers in managing risk. Nevertheless, given that the agricultural sector is often expected to provide 'public goods', the report adds that there is a case for financial support in certain circumstances, and given the synergies between agricultural and environmental policies they should not be treated as separate policy areas.The report proposed that Government should bring forward measures to help counter the effects of extreme weather events, and to work with the private sector to develop new financial tools (such as futures markets), improve training in their use, and provide tax measures, such as sheltered reserves and income averaging, to help individual farmers manage their cash flow. For smaller businesses these measures are of limited use. Futures contracts, for instance tend to be traded in larger quantities than might be appropriate to hedge risk for an individual producer, and working farmers are not likely to be on-line at times when the best deals may become available. Clubbing together in cooperative organisations is one partial solution, widely used in several EU countries, but the fact remains that income volatility is hugely damaging to the economic health of small businesses.

The justification for and extent to which support for national agricultural sectors grew in many developed countries, particularly after World War II, has been the subject of fierce debate for decades. Olivier de Schutter, former UN Special Rapporteur on the right to food (2008-14), argues that reaction to a perceived food crisis in world food supply in the two decades following that war led to massive government stimulation of the agriculture and food sectors in order to raise output and drive down prices[8]. This helped shape both the Green Revolution and the CAP and enabled large agri-food businesses effectively to control the agenda; '*these large actors have reason to oppose change today, so they can continue to flood markets with processed foods manufactured from the mountains of soy and corn that governmental subsidies encourage*'. Although this view may not be universally shared, there is little doubt that certain sectors of the agri-food business have profited royally, initially from protectionist policies, and later from helping steer the process of trade globalisation and tariff reduction in directions favouring their own interests.

A measure of the extent of corporate control of the world food trade was revealed in the Guardian newspaper in 2014[9]. At that time four large companies produced 58% of world seeds, four global firms accounted for 97% of poultry genetic R & D, and four more produced 60% of the agro-chemicals used by farmers. Since that date even further consolidation has taken place. According to the the Institute for Agriculture and Trade Policy (IATP)[10] the top five meat and dairy companies combined emit more greenhouse gases than Exxon, Shell or BP, and all of them have business plans which predict very significant volume growth in the next few years. I will return, in a later chapter, to speculate on how the dietary changes necessary for improving human health and helping mitigate climate change could meet opposition from powerful vested interests such as these. Inevitably this raises questions over individual governments' ability to control multi-national corporations, how global governance can be strengthened, and how to influence changes in corporate strategy through mobilising public opinion.

To achieve maximum profitability farmers must not only sell to the highest bidder but also take cognisance of those products or sectors which benefit from government support or subsidy. In the last chapter I set out the case for significant changes in the quantity and types of food that consumers should be encouraged to eat. Were such changes to occur, there would be consequences for what farmers could profitably produce. It is instructive to examine this from the viewpoint of an individual producer. His factory floor is a given area of land with particular characteristics, making it more suitable for some types of enterprise than others. If his farm is hilly, wet and has poor quality soil capable only of supporting rough grazing, his options are probably limited to extensive production of beef and sheep which have to be sold to lowland farms to finish ready for slaughter. He may consider planting trees, but that is unlikely to provide him or his family with full time employment or sufficient income. By contrast, consider a lowland farm on good, flat, stone free land with lower rainfall, but ample water reserves for crop growth. Here there may be a choice between many alternative enterprises. Some will demand particular skills or specialised investment, some may have high seasonal labour requirements and others may involve high risk, volatile yields and prices. Even on such farms good husbandry practice will demand a level of crop rotation to maintain fertility and keep down levels of soil borne crop diseases. Government support may be contingent on a range of crops being grown. Increasingly environmental regulation and restrictions on pesticides may limit his ability simply to choose the most profitable options.

In chapter 9 I indicated some of the rationale behind current moves to try to reduce consumers intake of sugar. For many years, when I was farming, my most profitable crop was sugar beet. The biggest areas of crops grown were the cereals, wheat and barley, but they are best grown alternately with break crops such as legumes, which tend to have variable yields and are often less profitable. So sugar beet was valuable as both a break crop and as a cash generator. Dietary change in future may reduce the market for sugar beet, and there are few alternatives with similar potential for profit. On a farm like mine such a change would not be terminal to the business. The picture might be very different on a specialised dairy farm, for instance, where the climate is not suitable for growing anything other than grass. Should the market for both dairy products and beef fall away then the business may not survive. Of course closure it is a reality to be faced by all businesses when they lose their market, but should an entire rural area be affected by such pressures, the community as a whole needs to consider whether some form of social support is justified.

In the UK, extremes of weather are unlikely to be as severe as in most other parts of the world. Even so, in the summer of 2018, the country endured the longest period of high temperatures and lack of rainfall since at least the 1960's. Where irrigation water was not available many crops withered and yields, particularly of fruits and vegetables, were severely reduced. Faster ripening of soft fruit and consequent lack of picking capacity meant that some good produce had to be left to rot in the field. Income from these high cost, high risk crops inevitably suffered. When Tim Lang, Professor of Food Policy at City University (University of London Centre for Food Policy) was asked in 2016 by Farmers Weekly[11] what we want from our food system post-Brexit, he said, *'it's four words, less farming, more horticulture'.* Farmers who had to deal with the summer of 2018 may think twice before changing their systems to follow Lang's advice unless some of their risk of loss is mitigated by governmental support, or by realistic prices which reflect the increased risks of crop failure.

New technology may not always bring with it reduced risk. I am a Trustee of a local, farmer owned arable crop research centre which recently staged an 'innovation day' for its members. Bill Clark, technical director of the National Institute for Agricultural Botany (NIAB), led a tour of trials of new wheat varieties to demonstrate their responses to different fungicide regimes. He emphasised the element of financial gamble in growing the highest yielding crops which were most responsive to fungicide treatment. *'They are profitable if you get it right'*, he said, *'but on a farm scale you won't always be able to do that, and when you get it wrong, you could lose significant yield and income'*[12]. His message was for farmers to consider balancing the risk of higher yielding varieties with lower yielding but more disease resistant ones. Farmers in general are pretty risk averse when it comes to adopting changes in technology or farming systems, and with good reason. Former US President, Dwight D Eisenhower once remarked *'Farming looks mighty easy when your plough is a pencil and you're 1000 miles from the cornfield'*. Changes which seem eminently sensible to government, economists, NGO's and scientists often seem less so when it comes to putting them into practice.

This is particularly the case when people have good intentions but lack local knowledge and experience. I recall my student days in the 1960's, one of my principal lecturers had been the chief scientific officer of the 1947 'groundnut scheme' in what is now Tanzania in East Africa. His job was to make a idea thought up in London work on the ground in Africa. Conceived as a means of filling the UK shortage of vegetable oil in the immediate post war period, whilst also developing 'colonial' land to be more productive, the British Government authorised expenditure of £25m over six years to cultivate 150,000 acres of scrubland to grow groundnuts. A combination of insufficient knowledge and 'buy-in' from the local population together with over optimistic direction from afar meant the scheme was a total disaster. It was terminated in 1951, having harvested only 2000 tons of groundnuts, costing £49m whilst turning the land into an unusable dustbowl.

A lot has been learned since then about how best to develop agriculture in poorer countries. Nowadays development experts stress the need for 'bottom up' planning, involving the cooperation of local people, local knowledge and local technologies wherever possible. People on the spot generally know their land better than anyone. They may not, however, have the knowledge or resource to exploit new technologies, and will be constrained by the risks involved in doing something new and different and breaking with traditional practices. In many cases there will be a lack of adequate finance and viable local markets, inadequate security of tenure to justify investment and unstable or corrupt government. Bridging those gaps is challenging, but necessary in order to be successful. Over the years a mass of literature has accumulated, examining the detailed factors contributing to the relative lack of progress in improving agricultural systems and productivity in some countries compared with others. Such knowledge helps efforts by donor countries to reduce world poverty, hunger and malnutrition.

It is important for readers in countries where most farming is already technically advanced to understand the lack of access to technical knowledge in many developing countries particularly in Africa, Asia and South America. Most farmers in the world are women. Globally there is an estimated 400 million women farmers[13], but in 90 countries local customs and laws inhibit womens access to land rights or water supplies. Those women who do have secure land rights are often well placed to farm effectively, save money and feed and educate their families. This can create a virtuous circle, where better nutrition and greater security encourages investment, improves educational standards, reduces land degradation and moves families out of poverty.

Improving rights to land for small family farms provided the engine to drive the post war economic miracles of Japan, South Korea and Taiwan[14]. As agricultural productivity soared it jump-started manufacturing and export businesses, in turn attracting investment capital into agri-food businesses. In more recent times, in China where rural land is normally held under collective ownership, several pilot schemes have allowed amalgamation of holdings to achieve economies of scale and greater management expertise. Some farmers have been allowed to mortgage their land in order to receive bank loans, because access to investment capital has been a major obstacle to farm improvement[15]. Interestingly, joint UK/China research[16] recently published shows that by increasing farm size, labour productivity improves and reduced pesticide and fertiliser use per unit area reflects greater technical knowledge and economic knowhow which accrues in larger farming businesses.

By contrast, in India, where the Green Revolution brought marked improvements to farm productivity and rural nutrition whilst reducing poverty during the latter part of last century, there is today a growing crisis of low farm incomes and stagnant productivity. The rural poverty rate is 25%, compared with14% in urban areas, and agricultural households account for 50% of India's poor[17]. The main problem is continued fragmentation of smallholdings through inheritance legislation. Since 1960 the average individual landholding has shrunk from 2.6ha (6.4acres) to 1.1ha. In addition, heavy reliance on variable monsoon rains makes yield levels unusually volatile[18]. Taxes on sale of land are heavy, disincentivising consolidation of holdings. Tenancy terms and laws governing access to water are often opaque and favourable to landlords. Bank loans and crop insurance have largely been the preserve of wealthy and more educated farmers, while the poor have had to resort to moneylenders.

Meanwhile the government is widely criticised for lavish spending on consumer subsidies, intended to reduce price volatility in staple crops. A 2015 survey[19] estimated that about 50% of wheat and sugar allocated by the government for the poor never reached them because of theft and innefficiencies in the distribution system. The subsidies encourage over cultivation of the few crops which the State does buy, especially wheat, rice and sugarcane, which are all thirsty crops, demanding a huge share of scarce and rapidly depleting water supplies. At the same time the Government controls or bans exports of these products, thereby capping producer prices[20]. Instead of a virtuous circle, India appears to have contrived a vicious circle involving greater expense for less reward.

Generally, in poorer countries, government food policy objectives are threefold: to increase food productivity; to develop effective markets; and to protect the poor and vulnerable from transitory food crises[21]. The political imperative of ensuring an adequate and affordable food supply to the poor encourages government interference with the free working of markets. As the illustration of India shows, this can reduce producer returns and discourage investment and innovation.There are no simple solutions. Many Indian farmers seeking to grow cash crops or increase yields through the purchase of hybrid seeds and fertilisers have found this to be a high risk strategy, which, in the event of crop failure can leave them in debt. In 2015 this resulted in a spate of farmer suicides[22].

In Africa US$1bn, or 30% of agricultural sector budgets was spent by the governments of 10 countries on large scale farm input subsidy programmes between 2000-2015[23]. The programmes, providing 30 -100% subsidies on the price of fertiliser and seed were targeted at reducing food insecurity and rural poverty. They were largely inneffective. A significant proportion of the funding ended up in the wrong hands. In Malawi, rural poverty actually increased after the policy was introduced in 2005, the result of poor targeting of recipients, inneffective governance and wide-spread corruption.

Since the turn of the century, in a liberalizing trading environment encouraged by globalisation, overt subsidisation of inputs or price support for specific crops has decreased significantly across the world. Nevertheless, most countries maintain a level of support for, or market interference in their agricultural sectors. The level of support may reflect the strength of the agricultural vote or consumer environmental and welfare concerns. It may address food price volatility and protection of domestic food supplies and, in developing nations, the extent of rural poverty and food insecurity. The level of government support ranges from almost zero in New Zealand, where almost all farm support was discontinued in 1985, to the highly protected Japanese market, and all levels in between. Most developing countries do not have the resources to compete with the more protectionist regimes, but almost all provide some form of market management. It is clear from the examples cited that some systems are less effective than others, and that as circumstances vary widely between countries, so too do the most appropriate forms of support or control, but all suffer from deficiencies of some kind or another.

A few generalised points can be made. Firstly, there is widespread consensus that excessive protectionism is bad, stifling development of international trade, often to the detriment of poorer countries. Support measures can mask market signals, slowing down reactions which could be beneficial in facing up to the likely effects of climate change. Interfering with international markets increases the likelihood of regional price volatility and discourages innovation. Secondly, if farmers are to benefit from measures to improve their productivity and responsiveness to markets and to improve their standard of living, governments must target their actions correctly, provide stability, long-term consistency of approach, and develop mutually beneficial trade agreements with other countries. Thirdly, the multiple aims of agricultural policy which vary in emphasis between countries, but which invariably include aspects of environmental and social policy as well as food, are too often put in separate 'boxes'. Health issues are more often than not completely missing from the equation. Policies develop separately and as a result the policy mix is often confused, contradictory, ill-fitting and inneffective.

Earlier I spent a little time discussing farming risks, which in many developing countries are extreme. Increased climatic risks leading to crop failures at regional scale are becoming more common. To meet this challenge there is a growing number of index linked insurance schemes, which pay out on the basis of pre-agreed and robustly defined area indices, rather than on specific individual claims. These can allow smallholder farmers to become more resilient to shocks which might otherwise put them out of business or even precipitate starvation. The existence of such schemes can give farmers the opportunity to access loans to invest in measures to increase productivity or diversify cropping with some degree of certainty that those loans can be repaid[24]. The spread of such schemes comes in parallel with more widely available mobile phone technology in developing countries, allowing payments to be made promptly online, and with improving data systems for forecasting weather and for confirming claims for damage done. Most schemes are subsidised both to encourage wide participation in an innovatory concept, and because full premiums would be unaffordable to many. India now administers the world's largest weather index insurance market, reaching tens of millions of farmers every year[ibid]. In general the farmer pays between 25-40% of the premium with the government subsidising the shortfall. Farmer trust needs to develop over time, but results have been encouraging. In Kenya, for example, an index based livestock insurance scheme providing insured pastoralists with payment in times of drought, is based on predicted rather than actual livestock deaths. It has been linked to a 50% drop in 'distress' sales of livestock to raise cash, a 33% reduced likelihood of having to eat significantly smaller meals, and a 33% reduction in dependence on food aid[25].

Specific indemnity insurance, available in most developed countries is too expensive for smallholder farmers and infeasible for insurance companies to administer. Yet as climate risks increase and individual premiums rise, the issue of wider insurance to help stabilise markets and reduce volatility of farm incomes is even being looked at by governments such as the UK. Both types of insurance are aimed at giving farmers greater incentive to invest in their businesses. For real progress to be made farmers need secure land tenure, relative price stability, access to research and development and stable government. They also need good practical advice ('extension') and good infrastructure (roads, markets, electrification, supply chains, etc.).

In the 1980's, when it became clear in the UK that farming had successfully risen to the challenge of raising domestic food production, the government of the day decided to withdraw from its role as provider of free technical information to farmers, a role which it had assumed since 1947. The whole system of nationally funded agricultural extension was privatised. In principle, farmers could access the same information and assistance by paying a commercial price for it. However, demand shrank considerably – farmers generally baulk at paying for advice, particularly when companies selling farm inputs such as fertiliser, agrochemicals and seeds are only too willing to fill the gap for free, (providing, of course, they can tempt farmers to buy their products). More than thirty years later there is an evident gap between so called 'blue sky' science and on-farm practice, particularly in areas of technology, such as soil science, where commercial companies have little to sell and no incentive to act as intermediaries.

I am in no doubt that the existence of independent and comprehensive extension services contributed greatly to the extraordinary rise in the productivity of UK agriculture between 1950-90. Of course, farmers can help themselves by funding the kind of work which links practical farming and academic research, and I am proud of my association, over many years, with one such initiative – a farmer owned research and extension centre in arable farming – which continues to provide relevant practical information to producers on the questions of most concern to them. But this kind of facility is unusual, even in developed countries. Developing countries invariably need investment from both government and private enterprise, not only in research, but in effective extension work too. Sadly, following the example of Western governments toward the end of the last century, many developing nations cut back on their expenditure, and aid agencies followed suit. From my own experience, 'before and after', many academic institutions teaching development studies moved away from teaching agriculture and into topics such as gender studies or conflict resolution. This was a mistake, yet to be fully rectified, because knowledge of agriculture is so important to the economies of many developing countries. Alumni returning to management positions in these countries should possess a strong foundation of knowledge about their primary industry.

Since the millenium there has been growing realisation in many countries that agricultural development is fundamental to overall economic development. Investment from governments, private companies and donors has begun to increase. Many of the earlier extension services were structured on a 'top down' approach, which was largely unsuccessful. More inclusive approaches, encouraging local community involvement, (and particularly womens groups), as well as other stakeholders in equal partnership, are now widespread.

Notably as the environmental impacts of agriculture become more understood around the world, extension agents have a wider responsibility for educating farmers in more sustainable agricultural techniques. Several African countries have responded to the challenge and are committing more funds and greater attention to their agricultural sectors. Problems of low productivity are particularly acute in Sub-Saharan Africa (SSA). In 1961 average cereal yields were around 1t/ha in SSA and 1.4t/ha in East Asia. By 2011 SSA yields had barely risen, while in East Asia they were more than 5t/ha[26].

A report from the Center on International Cooperation at New York University[27] suggests that '*many developing countries do not have the capacity or the will to impose accountable national governance, leaving a regulatory vacuum*'[28]. There are legitimate concerns that this vacuum is being filled by large agri-business and food corporations able to manage their business without government oversight. This highlights the considerable, and increasing power of private capital in the food and agriculture systems of developing countries. As the New York University report says[29], '*The challenge will be creating a public opinion environment where managers of food chain corporations see advantages and benefits in contributing to sustainable and socially responsible food production and development, while at the same time pursuing corporate goals established by their shareholders*'. I will return to this challenge in a later chapter.

Private investment is a crucial element for success in developing the rural infrastructure of poorer nations. Farmers themselves are, and will remain by far the largest source of investment in agriculture[30], but they will not invest adequately unless the investment climate is conducive, and this is fostered primarily by government. Corporate investors, sovereign funds and others investing in opportunities to create employment, enable technology transfer, or set up supply chains and storage capacity are very important, but need managing to ensure that individual property rights are not threatened and environmental and social concerns are fully taken into account.

Private investment usually favours newer technology and greater scale of operation in order to achieve efficiency and reduced cost. Governments, therefore, have a duty to protect the more vulnerable who may lose their livelihoods as a consequence. While particularly relevant to developing countries where no other options for employment may exist, the same economic pressures are felt globally.

In this chapter on farmers I have deliberately ranged from highly sophisticated farm businesses to subsistance smallholders. I have tried to demonstrate some of the major differences in the challenges they face, but also the similarities. All must find ways to deal with the vagaries of the weather and of a volatile market place over which they have very little control. Their businesses interfere with the natural world to an extent few other industries match. In consequence their management of it comes under particular scrutiny from the rest of society. In all societies farming has traditionally been the prime source of labour for other industries. Young people, in particular, leave the farm to work elsewhere. In consequence, farming becomes an industry for the middle aged and the old, and to some extent, the less educated. That makes change even more challenging. Almost everywhere, farm incomes are on average lower and more volatile than for comparable businesses. And increasingly, as global society becomes more urbanised, the gulf of understanding between farmers and the rest of society is growing.

In the next chapter I take a deeper look at government and society in the context of the food and environmental challenges raised earlier. What should their roles be in addressing change? How difficult will it be to stimulate action both nationally and internationally?

# Chapter 11

# Government and Society

'Not everything that is faced can be changed, but nothing can be changed until it is faced'.

*James Baldwin, American novelist, in New York Times 1962)*

Olivier de Schutter (see chapter 10)[1] believed that it was decisive government action which stimulated massive changes to agricultural productivity following the end of World War II. Agri-food businesses in wealthy countries expanded the range of consumer products and led the revolution in eating habits and consumer lifestyles we know so well today. These changes took more than one generation (25-30 years) to work through so it seems likely that if governments try to change consumer habits once more, that change will also take considerable time. It is a similar story for all of the challenges discussed in this book, but the longer we put off the necessary actions to deal with them the greater the risk to the health and well being of future generations.

It is now clear that many of the challenges will be faced first and most critically by those living in low income countries. Global warming effects are distributed unevenly, affecting temperate regions least. Low income societies are more vulnerable, having less resilience to economic shocks and natural disasters[2]. Some of these countries will also be the ones where population is growing fastest and where governments are struggling to 'catch up' the West in terms of economic development. They face the dilemma of being, at the same time, both victim and perpetrator of environmental degradation and climate change.

Asia is an example, where the consumption of coal grew by 3.1% a year between 2006 – 2016, making up almost 75% of world demand for this most polluting of fossil fuels[3]. Most was used to produce electricity.

95

In India, planned demand for electricity is forecast to triple between 2012 and 2030. Pleas from developed countries for India to reduce its reliance on coal have been met with counter claims of 'carbon imperialism'. In other words, 'you expanded your economies on the back of cheap polluting energy in the past, so you do not have the moral right to lecture us'. It is an understandable position, particularly when the US, the largest economy in the world, officially refutes man-made climate change and threatens to withdraw from the Kyoto agreement, in which almost every other country has indicated a willingness to take some action on climate change.

China, the world's largest consumer of coal, built much of its recent economic expansion on polluting fossil fuels. By 2030 China is predicted to produce 16bn tonnes of greenhouse gases annually[4] which is four times the entire world output in 1900. Although it has now set enormously ambitious targets for expansion of wind and solar power, backed by government incentive schemes[5], in the hope of combining environmental sustainability with profit from being an early innovator in new technology it is possible that China has left it too late to avoid severe domestic problems. The north China plain, the country's bread basket, where irrigated agriculture has expanded enormously, is at risk of more frequent and deadly heatwaves, which could make working and living there intolerable[6].

Governments role, for good or bad is fundamental to the future of the planet. The World Economic Forum 2017 Global Risks Report[7] notes intensifying nationalist sentiment across the world, despite the evident need to improve global cooperation in managing change. Among its 2017 top five risks are changing climate, ageing populations and increased polarization of societies. And it maintains that *the confluence of risks around water scarcity, climate change, extreme weather events and involuntary migration, remains a potent cocktail and risk multiplier, especially in the world economy's more fragile environmental and political contexts*.

Existing international institutions are relatively weak and do not cooperate sufficiently well despite many of them being under the umbrella of the United Nations. Some of the most important institutions connected with food and agriculture are FAO (Food and Agriculture Organisation), WFP (World Food Programme), IFAD (International Fund for Agricultural Development, CGIAR (Consultative Group for International Agricultural Research, UNEP (United Nation Environmental Programme), OECD (Organisation for Economic Cooperation and Development), WHO

(World Health Organisation), IPCC (Inter-governmental Panel on Climate Change and World Bank. There are many other smaller and subsidiary bodies. In 2016 a comprehensive review by von Braun and Birner[8] looked at how these organisations might work together to improve international governance of agricultural development, food and nutrition security. They recommended that developing countries, or a committed group of nations, under the auspices of the UN or G20, should create a structure to coordinate certain closely inter-related set of priorities. These are natural resource management related to biodiversity, water and soils, climate change adaptation and mitigation, trade regimes, food reserves and related global information, competition policy and standards for foreign direct investment, international research and innovation in food and agriculture, responding to and preventing food and nutrition emergencies, and transboundary food safety and health related investments and standards. Currently in all of these areas of activity von Braun and Birner identified gaps in provision and a lack of coordination between existing bodies. For instance, CGIAR is a valuable organisation for developing countries agricultural research, but represents only 4% of total global agricultural research spending[9]. Agriculture, until recently, was largely ignored within the climate conferences of the UN Framework Convention on Climate Change (UNFCC) despite being a major contributor of greenhouse gas emissions. Rules based trade is essential for food security and is largely administered under the WTO (World Trade Organisation). But WTO, founded in 1995, has made limited progress in liberalising and reforming this sector of the global economy, compared to most other sectors. This organisation and others have been widely accused by smaller nations of being controlled by the more powerful states, such as the USA, (despite contrary claims by the Trump White House). As a result, regulatory agreements are generally more favourable to larger states, and, by implication, to the powerful vested interests in those countries able to influence their governments policies. As Professor Sir John Marsh[10] comments in relation to the rules governing exploitation of natural resources, where international institutions are often impotent to act against unwilling national governments, *'Governments faced by environmental problems that are geographically or temporally remote are likely to give greater weight to competing demands from local, well organised pressure groups. Retaining power depends on those whose votes will determine their own continuation in office'*.

The 2014 United Nations Conference on Trade and Development

(UNCTAD) report[11] argued for *'effective policy instruments ... enabling countries to favour the real economy over financial interests (and) puts sustainability ahead of short term gains ...'* Economic globalization, which became the dominant paradigm from the 1980's led to a huge expansion of economic integration between countries, leading to a 'world market' for goods and services. It contributed massively to economic growth across the world as liberalisation of markets allowed goods to be traded more easily and cheaply. Three hundred years ago, Scottish economist Adam Smith wrote his famous book *The Wealth of Nations,* in which he made the case for free trade for the benefit of all. Almost 100 years later, another British economist, David Ricardo, set out his 'theory of comparative advantage' where free trade allows countries to specialise in what they are good at producing. In this way all, on average, should be better off. The overall global prosperity that has been generated over the last half century as a result of following these maxims cannot be denied. It has allowed most people in the world to benefit from a higher standard of living and it has removed millions from poverty and destitution. But it has also been the engine for over-exploitation of world resources and is a major contributor to global challenges which are the subject of this book.

Globalisation has other negative effects, which go some way to explaining why so many people now seek to return to various forms of protectionism. It puts at risk the livelihoods of those who are unable to compete effectively with imported products; it contributes to growing inequality in many societies; the effectiveness of national policies tends to be weakened, very significantly in some instances, especially by financial globalisation. It is a current truism that 'if the dollar sneezes, the world catches a cold'. Particularly in developing countries financial instability, originating elsewhere in the world, can easily destabilise their own economies[12].

Globalisation also affects the ability of countries to raise taxes – market liberalism has led to a global economy which encourages tax competition, pushing countries into a 'race to the bottom' to attract industrial investment by offering lower taxation to multi-national companies. Legitimate tax avoidance has been spectacularly lucrative for many multi-national companies able to domicile themselves in the country offering the lowest tax rates. Huge companies such as Google, Amazon and Apple have been accused by politicians of paying insufficient tax, and the EU has proposed taxation on the basis of turnover rather than profit, because it can more easily be linked to a geographic area. Finance led globalisation has encouraged a proliferation of offshore financial centres and tax havens that provide various means of tax avoidance on a massive scale[13]. In 2016 the media made much of the leaking of the 'Panama Papers', originating from the Panamanian law firm Mossad Fonseca. The documents contained personal information about wealthy individuals and public officials which was previously unpublished. Reporters found numerous examples of 'shell corporations' used for illegal purposes, including fraud, tax evasion and evading international sanctions. According to the Overseas Development Institute (ODI)[14] for every $1 Africa receives in foreign aid, it loses $1.30 through illicit transfers. Euractiv[15] calculates the loss to be a staggering 5.4% of Sub Saharan African GDP.

A problem common to developed and developing countries alike is that governments everywhere are faced with new and growing demographic, health, social and environmental challenges which will require significantly more public expenditure than in the past. I am reminded of words by my favourite economist, when I was a student back in the 1960's. J K Galbraith wrote a famous book called *The Affluent Society*[16] in which he noted with concern the *'private affluence and public squalor'* in the America of his day. His phrase remains prescient in the light of current challenges. While some modern economists cling to the belief that the free market should be allowed to solve all problems with minimal government interference, it is increasingly clear that the market cannot, and, equally importantly, will not do so without very significant direction, investment and consistency of purpose from government. In economic parlance, the role of government is to correct market failures, but as the topics covered in this book demonstrate, these failures are deep and widespread. Yet governments are constrained not only by short-term views of their electorates but also by the level of taxation they feel they can raise, thereby limiting their power to manage change. Multi-national corporate power also threatens government sovereignty to act in national interest.

In 2005 the UK government commissioned Sir Nicholas Stern to produce a report on the economics of climate change, and what might be done to adapt to it and mitigate its effects, particularly from a UK perspective. In 2007 he published *'The Economics of Climate Change: The Stern Review'*[17]. The book played a significant role in making the issue of climate change better known and more widely debated than before. It attracted critics and 'climate deniers', as I noted in Chapter 2, but its main message was clear. Government needed to take urgent action if the costs of climate change were not to spiral beyond reach, particularly for the next generation. It held out the relatively optimistic view that our economic system could carry on very much as before, provided that the world took seriously the need to change quickly from polluting and destroying 'brown growth' to non-polluting and sustainable 'green growth'[18]. All economies would need to take a relatively short term 'hit' to their GDP's – perhaps as little as 1% annually, whilst delaying action might imply costs as much as 20% of GDP annually, which Lawson[19] (see chapter 2) and other climate change sceptics derided as fanciful, particularly criticising the discount rates used to calculate future costs.

Discount rates are most usually the assumed interest rates applied to competing investment proposals, in order to analyse which are most cost effective. They allow comparison of the 'net present value' of investments to give an indication to business managers where limited cash resources should be spent. Clearly, the bigger the discount applied, and the longer the payback period, the less attractive will be an investment made now, for future return. The concept, when applied to national investment over the longer term is more questionable. It is critiqued in a book by US economist Tyler Cowan[20.] *'Few governments do everything they can to promote economic growth in the more distant future – the emphasis is generally short term'.* His point is that if we artificially discount the importance of the future then current action will not seem imperative. Lawson criticised Stern for applying too low a discount rate to current investment in climate change mitigation measures. Stern used a 1% rate, but even that is arguably too high when we consider that we are effectively gambling with the lives and lifestyles of future generations. As Cowan says[21] *'Under any positive discount rate, one life today is worth more than 1 million lives in the (distant) future'.* Discounting for the risk of something not happening as expected is clearly reasonable, but where the risk of inaction potentially leads to irreversible change which threatens future generations, it does not seem an appropriate measure on which to base decisions.

Although economies as a whole in Stern's scenario might continue much as normal, the required upheaval to some economic sectors would be very significant. In particular, any industry or activity reliant on the use of fossil fuels would undergo radical change, and the unexploited reserves of the fuels themselves would become 'stranded assets' with no further value. This alone would create upheaval in financial markets, with knock-on effects for everyone whose pension income is reliant on stock market performance. Our system of market economics is a treadmill. For businesses to succeed in a competitive environment what matters is not how fast they adapt to change, but whether they do it faster than anyone else. The profit motive stimulates the search for better, cheaper and novel products through innovation and what economists term 'creative destruction', but in parallel, the market for these goods depends on maintaining an expanding consumer demand. Together these factors drive growth in the economy, and growth allows people to pay themselves more, and to invest their savings in creating more jobs and more goods.

Although this paints a very simplistic picture of the workings of capitalism it is evident that within this model there appears very little room to incorporate concepts of sustainability – that is, where no more resources are extracted than are put into the system. As Tim Jackson puts it in his book 'Prosperity without Growth'[22], 'The throwaway society is not so much a consequence of consumer greed as a structural prerequisite for survival (of the economic system)'. But in a world where we have already exceeded some planetary boundaries (see Chapter 2) and are dangerously close to exceeding more, and where our environment is under threat as never before, should we actively promote a system of living which implies constant increase in our consumption? Asking such a question is anathema to most economists, politicians, businessmen and consumers alike. Such 'revolutionary' thinking goes far further than the 'green economy' proposed by Stern, and questions his view that capitalism, as we know it, can continue within a green and sustainable framework.

Given that even Stern's relatively modest recommendations are far from universally agreed or acted upon some 10 years after their publication, it seems unlikely that the entire edifice of modern capitalism will be torn down anytime soon. But we do urgently need to make progress toward reducing overall growth in material consumption. In 'economist speak' this is termed 'decoupling'[23], implying movement towards 'smart', 'green', 'sustainable' growth. In order to do this, at the very least, we need to impose clear resource and environmental limits on our exploitation of global resources. We need to discourage consumers from 'keeping up with the Jones's', and we need to move away from GDP (Gross Domestic Product) as a measure of economic progress. People instinctively know that modern lifestyles are deeply irresponsible, but we are all caught up in the treadmill. As Kenneth Boulding commented at a hearing of the US Congress in

1973,' *anyone who believes that exponential growth can go on for ever is either a madman or an economist'.*

GDP was a measurement originally proposed by the economist John Maynard Keynes to help understand the capacity of the UK economy to build equipment for the coming World War II[24]. Since then the measure has been developed piecemeal in an attempt to capture as much data as possible about the output of an economy. (In 2003, for example, it included income from selling recreational drugs and paid sex work – which, in Britain added 0.7% to GDP!). It is, however, a poor measure of prosperity and unreliable as a gauge of production. It does not measure innovation in many areas, does not account for quality of consumption, nor externalities (factors not priced into production costs). So it takes little account of asset depreciation, pollution or environmental damage. Indeed, it treats 'planetary plunder' as something which adds to income rather than destroys the 'family silver'. Moreover, prosperity is about much more than material pleasures. As the late Robert Kennedy, in a speech at the University of Kansas in 1968[25] remarked, '*(GDP) measures neither our wit or our courage, neither our wisdom or our learning, neither our compassion or our duty to our country. In short, everything except that which makes life worthwhile'.*

In chapter 7 I referred to the concept of 'natural capital' – often also referred to as 'ecosystem services' to indicate the benefits the natural world provides, such as clean air and water or insects and unseen soil fauna which support global food production and which are not credited in standard forms of accounting. Governments and economists until recently appeared largely blind to our dependency on the environment, assuming that mankind can continue to exploit and abuse natural systems without consequences. Recognition of climate change, biodiversity loss, air pollution in our cities and plastic pollution of our seas has changed public attitudes, but experts have been slow to suggest other than partial solutions. Some, such as George Monbiot, the environmental campaigner, take the purist approach that nature is quite separate from the economic system, and that trying to put a monetary value on natural processes is morally wrong and potentially counter productive leading to the wholesale destruction of nature for profit[26]. But a riposte from researchers at the Oxford Martin School, University of Oxford, points out[27], '*we urgently need to start addressing the underlying economic structures that are incentivising destruction'.* We need systems and techniques to handle that data so that monetary transactions at all levels can begin to incorporate the currently unassigned value of natural capital within the day to day economy.

Work commissioned by UNEP (United Nations Environmental Programme) under the title '*The Economics of Ecosystems and Biodiversity*' *(TEEB)*[28] shows that of the 20 global economic sectors by region having the greatest damaging impact in monetary terms 11 are directly applicable to agriculture, including cattle ranching in South America (ranked 2nd), and wheat and rice farming in South Asia (4th, 5th). Three more are closely related, namely water supply in South Asia, West Asia and North Africa (9th, 12th, 17th). Although this ranking highlights the biggest global issues, it should be evident that wherever our activities impinge on the natural world there will be consequences which require understanding and proper evaluation. Hence, Defra in the UK is seeking ways to incorporate payment to farmers for ecosystem services within future environmental schemes. This is very much an exercise in putting a toe in the water for the UK government. There is no indication, as yet, that it is considering policies which build environmental costs into food prices. Logically, a more comprehensive way of incorporating externality costs to society could be devised by the public paying more for public health care, prevention of air or water pollution and improved diets. Until a new and agreed framework of economic theory and practice can be agreed nationally and inter-nationally, this is probably a step too far. Other types of measures by governments will continue to be needed to reflect the changes in behaviour required from businesses and consumers alike.

Implicit within arguments for greater accountability of externality costs is the need for better understanding of the complex inter-related nature of economic systems. In practice governments generally compart-mentalise policy and decision making. A 2016 research paper led by the Tyndall Centre for Climate Change[29] looked at current UK policies on water, energy and food. It concluded they '... *are too fragmented to effec-tively tackle global challenges'. For example, 'there is little integration between recommended diets and the policies of growing plants and animals, or between agriculture and forestry'*, and '... *by exhausting resources at a faster rate than they can be replenished (such as soil fertility and clean water), and by not mitigating climate change, the current generation is robbing future generations of the ecosystem services it has itself enjoyed'*. The paper recommends a radical overhaul of the current system of policy and decision making within a broad cross sectoral framework of data on ecosystem services, which does not simply focus on those areas which are easier to study and quantify.

While there are evident deficiencies in the workings of the UK government, the problems are far more deep seated in many other countries, particularly those where systems of government are less well developed. Economist and Daily Telegraph columnist Roger Bootle[30] questioned whether countries in Sub Saharan Africa can achieve the rapid growth they need to pull themselves out of poverty in future. He commented '... *at bottom, what really matters for economic development is governance. If a country does not invest, its workforce remains poorly educated. If markets are not allowed to function properly and if government is corrupt and innefficient, then the likelihood is that growth will be slow'*. In the introduction to a conference organised by the Overseas Development Institute in 2014[31] I noted comments made by a seasoned commentator on African affairs that, in his experience, '*evidence based policy making rarely results in policies based on such evidence. It has more to do with instruments to retain power'*.

Such comments reflect the reality that global change is slow, uneven and beset by deep rooted problems which have more to do with human frailties than with the complexity of the real challenges which face us. Tasks such as developing a global system of accounting for ecosystem services face enormous barriers of vested interest, venality and lack of understanding. They will only succeed if there is strong and clear leadership at both national and international levels together with consistency of approach over a long period. Major global challenges should transcend adversarial or short term politics. It would be easy, looking at the world today to be pessemistic over the outcome, but I prefer to follow Archbishop Desmond Tutu of South Africa. When asked whether he was an optimist he replied '*I am a prisoner of hope'*.

In my more than 30 years experience of dealing with UK government departments and with the EU Commission, each being professional and having high ethical standards, I noted a tendency for them to become embroiled in short term fixes and the minutiae of day to day practice to the detriment of setting and sticking to a long term strategy. That may be partly due to the necessity of dealing with lobbyists and NGO's who are motivated to press their own one sided views. Referring again to economist J.K. Galbraith, in another of his books called '*The Anatomy of Power*'[32], he succinctly pictures the relative power of lobbyists in this way: '*If the organisation seeking submission to its purposes is internally strong... then its ability to win external submission is proportionally greater'.* In other words, single issue pressure groups are more often effective in getting what they want than those organisations with a broad spectrum of interests. Throughout this book I seek to make the case for a broad brush approach to complex challenges, and it is salutary to realise that this is 'politically' a very difficult feat to achieve. I recall a conversation, some years ago, with an older colleague who was then chairman of a government agency concerned with environmental protection. He let slip that his door was open to well over 100 different organisations all trying to bend his ear to their point of view. *'In my office'* he said, *'they are all reasonable people. But when they go outside and talk to the Press they are b......s'.* Single issues are easier for most people to understand, and simplistic messages are often more persuasive in persuading people to part with their money. Extremists, though small in number tend to punch above their weight in getting their views across, as I know to my cost in trying to deal, over many years, with several animal rights groups, which simply refused to listen to anything other than their own point of view. Sadly, the rise of social media in recent years has worsened the tendency of all kinds of interest groups to polarize. By deliberately producing algorithms to link those with similar interests, the result is to reinforce existing viewpoints, reduce understanding of alternative positions and threaten a balanced society.

Despite all of these difficulties the role of government is crucial in leading innovation and change. In her book *'The Entrepreneurial State'* Mariana Mazzucato[33] clearly demonstrates the crucially important role of the state in stimulating and nurturing new technologies such as clean energy and biotechnology. It is much more than the limited role of correcting 'market failures' propounded by right wing economists and politicians. Without considerable public finance, investment incentives, loan guarantees and provision of markets and the stimulation and financing of innovative and 'risky' research and early stage development, many of the most innovative technologies of the last half century would not have reached the market place. Mazzucato demonstrates that commercial appetite for risk is distinctly limited and venture capitalists look for returns in much shorter time periods than may be required to commercialize fully a new industry such as wind energy or some forms of biotechnology.

This leadership role of the State does not simply relate to identification of novel areas of activity and to public finance of R and D. It has responsibilities to initiate appropriate change in the habits of business and consumers where market forces and public appetites appear to be against the longer term public good. These responsibilities are implicit in all the arguments rehearsed earlier in this chapter, but they continue to be constantly debated and challenged because they affect the lives and livelihoods of everyone. Several governments have tried to introduce 'sin taxes', particularly on products high in sugar. As I noted in chapter 9, there have been some successes, but also some apparent failures. The point of such taxes is to make unhealthy goods relatively more expensive, but as a consequence, because poorer people spend a greater proportion of their income on food, and buy more of the cheaper and less healthy products, they tend to bear a greater burden of the cost. So what begins as a means of deterring people from harmful behaviour and reducing the cost of bad health to the public purse, ends up creating a potential social problem. Similarly, applying a global carbon tax, (a levy on emissions) or expanding biofuel plantations or planting trees on a major scale to help curb climate change could push up the price of food and put millions more people at risk of hunger, particularly in poorer countries[34]. The researchers who came to this conclusion emphasised the need to be flexible in designing much needed policies to mitigate climate change whilst minimising the anti-social consequences. They suggested a better alternative would be to reduce emissions from the production process and impose a tax on red meat and dairy products. But that brings us back to issues of personal freedom of choice and the uneven burden on society that such a tax would imply. To counter this criticism, Switzerland calls its carbon taxes 'levies' and the government pays back two thirds of receipts to households and businesses and spends the other third on 'green' investments[35].

The complexity of choices faced by governments is clearly demonstrated by work undertaken by the McKinsey Global Institute in 2014[36]. After analysing a whole raft of different measures to tackle the problem of obesity, the authors concluded that, '*No single solution creates sufficient impact to reverse obesity: only a comprehensive, systemic programme of multiple interventions is likely to be effective.*' Amongst the list of interventions (in order of impact) are portion control, reduction in availability of high calorie foods and beverages, weight management programmes, parental education, school curriculum change and healthy meals. Interestingly, taxation comes much further down the list. So if this single issue of obesity is to be tackled effectively it needs cross-cutting and coordinated measures from many areas of government – a point made earlier in this chapter. Not only that, but the authors also stress that alongside government, commitment is needed from employers, educationalists, retailers, restaurants and food and beverage manufacturers.

To what extent there is 'buy-in' of these various changes from business is questionable. I touched on this area in chapter 9, making reference to the enormous sums spent by the food industry to market its products compared with the amount available to the disease prevention budget of the World Health Organisation (WHO)[37] – ($40bn in 2015 against $8bn). The power of the meat industry to sway their governments is also noted by Godfray[38] referring to the powerful influence of the USA and South American beef exporting countries on WTO rules, which, for instance, forced Samoa, one of the most obese nations on earth, to reverse a ban on fatty meat imports introduced as an obesity control measure. And, as mentioned in Chapter 10, every one of the big meat and dairy companies globally is budgeting for significant expansion in meat eating, whilst, at the same time claiming they will achieve ambitious emission reduction targets[39]. It is unclear how they can meet both targets simultaneously.

Yet there is cause for some optimism. The head of Danone, one of the biggest multinational food companies, now rejects the Anglo-Saxon concept that companies exist primarily to maximise returns to shareholders. Instead, he believes the company has a duty to provide healthy food to as many mouths as possible, benefitting suppliers, consumers and shareholders alike[40]. Others, whilst not being so outspoken admit that companies should serve a social purpose. Larry Fink, founder and CEO of the world's biggest asset manager, Blackrock, mailed all companies in which Blackrock has a shareholding, saying they should no longer focus solely on profit[41]. Other fund managers, such as Legal and General Investment Management, want companies to take into account in their business planning internationally recognised targets such as the Paris agreement on limiting global warming below 2 degrees C. More and more companies are voluntarily committing themselves to membership of organisations such as the World Business Council for Sustainable Development. In a movement which began in the United States, city authorities across the world are starting to act unilaterally, to protect their populations from air pollution by banning diesel powered cars, safeguarding water resources, legislating on fast food outlets and many other areas of concern where markets are not working for the common good and national governments are unwilling or too slow to act.

There is often a significant financial liability for companies which follow through on their commitments, particularly in the fiercely competitive environment of food retailing in developed economies. The sector is driven by a model that depends on continually growing the value of consumer purchases. Volume sales make up for low margins, encouraging excessive levels of consumption and waste. Humans are psychologically programmed to prefer high calorie foods and the food industry has expanded dramatically by providing a continuous stream of novel products designed to maximise added value to the manufacturer and retailer. Not unexpectedly, the industry so far has been reluctant to agree to measures to curb consumption. While paying lip service to environmental costs retailers are conscious that most food purchases are price driven. Unless the sector acts together as one, or government imposes regulations, individual companies are unlikely to take significant steps to raise prices to reflect environmental costs, or to try to change consumer buying patterns to reflect healthier lifestyles. Nonetheless, changes do occur slowly, often in response to consumer pressure, and this in turn may be influenced by government or the media. In combination, these factors can occasionally lead to relatively swift response, as exemplified by current moves to reduce plastic food packaging in the UK.

Throughout this chapter it will be evident that primary producers – farmers – have little real influence over changes that will occur to the food system. I often use the phrase, 'farmers are price-takers, not price-makers'. In other words, their collective power in the market place is very small, particularly in developed countries where most of the capital (and profit) is made beyond the farm gate. What they grow, or what livestock they rear will depend on decisions taken elsewhere in the economy. It is little wonder that most farmers concentrate on new technologies aimed at improving their own productivity in order to remain in a business where it is in every-one elses interest to keep food prices down. To some extent the arguments in this book for dramatically changing current forms of agriculture will wash over working farmers because they are at the mercy of these changes over which they will have little influence. Healthy eating trends and rising concerns over animal welfare in the wealthier countries of Europe and America have stimulated efforts by manufacturers to produce meat-free alternatives to meat. Livestock farmers in future may face declining demand for their products in these markets for reasons unconnected with the climate change arguments made earlier in this book. Nevertheless, I think it important both that they have a better understanding of the pressures on their industry, and that the general public have some greater understanding of the role of farmers and of the difficulties they face. And because so many future challenges are global in scope it is important for all to appreciate the differences and the similarities between farmers in different parts of the world, and the problems faced by world leaders in trying to bring together solutions to a mass of interconnected challenges of which future food supply is only one. The next three chapters seek to pull together the multiple strands woven into this book, and speculate on whether solutions can or will be found.

# Chapter 12

# Problems and Solutions 1?

'I can calculate the movement of the stars, but not the madness of men.'

*Isaac Newton* (who lost a fortune speculating on the South Sea Bubble)

Can the human race use the short time available wisely to prevent potential catastrophe? It depends to a large extent on the capacity of the majority to behave rationally. Unfortunately a number of behavioural studies indicate that rationality and logic are often insufficient. In his *'Comment'* section in the Times newspaper, journalist Max Hastings[1] cited work by Ohio State University researchers who in 2015 tested different reactions to news stories by liberal and conservative voters in America. They found both groups tended to discount any science which contradicted their existing beliefs, often questioning the validity of research which presented data unpalatable to their own views. In reality, it seems most of us tend to look at solutions, decide whether we like them, and then work backwards to decide whether there really is a problem in the first place.

That makes it hard for political leaders to take decisive actions on measures where voters are asked to pre-pay costs or forego current benefits in order to defer or prevent longer term consequences, (which some argue might not happen anyway). A depressing article in the Washington Post[2] around the time of the IPCC COP24 meeting in Katowice, Poland, reported a Gallup survey asking Americans to name the most important problems facing the country. Environmental issues failed to score above 3% even though the climate talks were ongoing. The same article cited work by the Pew Research Centre which found the public ranked Climate Change 18th out of 19 possible top priorities for the US Congress to address urgently. In a demonstration of partisan behaviour in practice, Democrat voters were 4 times more likely to consider Climate Change important than Republicans.

Worryingly, right wing groups and politicians the world over increasingly denigrate measures to combat climate change. In Germany the right wing opposition Party, Alternative for Germany (AfD) calls climate change a hoax. In the US President Trump tweeted support for the Paris fuel tax protesters and is actively seeking to roll back US environmental legislation designed to address climate change and promote biodiversity.

In Brazil a new populist President has publicly stated he will encourage further exploitation of the Amazon forests rather than preserve them for the long term good of humanity. Although wealthy nations bear heavy responsibility for past climate and environmental damage, it is in the fast growing emerging economies where most damage is being done today. Palm oil plantations in South East Asia and cattle ranches in Brazil have decimated natural forests. Chinese industrialisation has massively increased global greenhouse gas emissions and polluted large areas of soil and water. In countries like the UK we should be under no illusion that any actions we might take will have little effect if the rest of the world fails to follow suit.

Following the world recession of 2008, the rate of economic growth slowed down. Since then inequality between the 'haves and the have nots' has increased in several countries. This reflects in wider levels of voter dissatisfaction and a rise in support for nationalist and extremist parties. The aggressive and unrestrained use of economic nationalism by the Trump administration in the US is the polar opposite of what is required to face climate change. Weakened governments driven to more protectionist policies could precipitate another economic crisis. This recession could be particularly 'toxic', leading to further political polarization and factionalism.

Arguably, the meteoric rise of social media communication adds to the current polarisation of political views. Algorithms on platforms such as Facebook and Twitter are designed to link together people expressing similar interests and views, thereby encouraging and sustaining particular viewpoints to the exclusion of others. Their power to manipulate views, and to sow confusion and dissent is harnessed by hostile governments and commercial interests. Populists use such media to misinform, and to spread anti-establishment rhetoric in which 'experts' are not to be trusted. Such is the power of these platforms that news, whether real or 'fake' spreads quickly. I recall a report on BBC World service radio that six out of ten people only read the headlines of stories before passing them on to others. A University of Colorado study published in *Nature: Human Behaviour*[3] asked 2000 EU and US citizens how well they understood the science of genetic modification. Those most strongly opposed to GMO's believed they had a good understanding, but when tested on their knowledge, they clearly did not. This is consistent with previous research on the psychology of extremism, which suggests that changing peoples minds first requires them to acknowledge what they don't know.

With all this bad news, is it possible that common sense may yet prevail? There are indeed some green shoots here and there. In Chapter 11 I noted that some financiers are beginning to move markets toward a 'greener' future. Investors such as the Church Commissioners in the UK target much of their investment investment into environmentally friendly asset classes. Some companies are developing strategies in the light of concerns for the planet, but motivated also by self preservation. Climate change directly affects the risks that firms face, from rising sea levels, threat of carbon taxes, increased insurance costs and the future likelihood of 'stranded assets'. Shareholders increasingly expect companies to plan for climate change and to develop a social conscience.

Mrs Thatcher's favourite economist, Milton Friedman, opined that the sole purpose of business, so long as it played by the rules, was to use resources and engage in activities designed to increase profits. Modern economists support the view that other factors, including social and environmental ones, should be incorporated into company accounts[4&5]. This could be achieved, admittedly with some difficulty, by putting a value on environmental and social costs, when calculating taxation and distribution of dividends. The economists proposals have much in common with my suggestion in chapter 11 for the development of a new economic system to take into account all levels of 'externalities'. Practical or not, at this time, it is at least encouraging to see an awakening realisation that our present economic system is not fit for purpose for the more challenging world that awaits us.

While debate continues on this topic a number of Governments around the world have made firm commitments to meet the climate change challenge. Although many are behind the curve in terms of fulfilling those commitments there is growing realisation of the need for faster progress, as demonstrated by the number of countries who have now committed to target dates to phase out all diesel motor vehicles. In the UK, and with cross party support, the independent Committee on Climate Change was created in 2008, (see chapter 2). This Committee in 2019 produced detailed recommendations for each UK economic sector, reflecting increasing concern from the scientific community for urgent action.

Although this book primarily considers the 20-25% of GHG's emitted by the food and agriculture sectors, the issues raised cannot be separated from the overall need to reduce GHG's across all sectors and globally. Till now, the brunt of efforts in the UK, as elsewhere, have been borne by the energy sector, and to a lesser extent transport and construction. The agriculture and food sectors and consumers must now play a more significant role.

One of the earliest and most authoritative publications setting out the complexity of this task was the UK Government commissioned *Foresight Report on the Future of Food[6] 2011*. Many other reports have followed calling for concerted policy responses across a range of disciplines. Recent instances include an academic workshop convened by the UK based Global Food Security Programme[7] and a World Resources Institute Report[8]. Both reports recommend reducing growth in demand for food, including a reduction in food waste and limiting consumption, particularly of red meat. Also recommended is efficient intensification of food production to allow 'land sparing', thereby freeing up more land for biodiversity and the protection of natural ecosystems. Linking food systems with health rather than on yields per se prioritises well-being and again points to the need for urgent development of true cost accounting. FAO published a detailed paper in January 2016[9] linking better, more healthy dietary patterns with low environmental impacts. The document pleads for consistent and well publicised dietary guidelines and for strong governmental support to encourage consumers to change their habits. Guidelines in this area are largely the preserve of health Ministries at present. The need for much wider coordination of expert opinion from different areas of expertise is evident. *Food in the Anthropocene: the EAT Lancet Commission on healthy diets from sustainable food systems[10]* does examine the food system in an holistic way, and recommends changes in food production systems, international and national commitment to healthy diets and reduction of food waste. It also recommends strong and coordinated governance of land and oceans, and gives me an opportunity to briefly consider what is happening to our seas and oceans and to comment on the global fishing industry. The maltreatment of our oceans is one subject crying out for international regulation and effective oversight to stop unsustainable practices.

The UK House of Commons environmental audit committee reported in 2018[11] on the 'triple whammy' of threats to the ocean of warming, deoxygenation and acidification. Ocean warming is causing huge changes to life in the oceans, the most well publicised being the dramatic loss of coral reefs, which are considered the rain-forests of the ocean because of the abundance of marine life they support. Scientists now believe that 93% of all the heat resulting from extra greenhouse gas in the atmosphere is absorbed by the oceans[12]. When this figure is fed into computer climate models the 'match' between the models and observed changes in ocean temperatures to date is very close, implying that warming is accelerating at a rate 40% higher than was previously thought.

Deoxygenation of coastal waters, largely resulting from pollution by fertilisers and organic material run-off from agriculture and industry, is an increasingly severe problem. As a result, vast areas of what once were productive fishing grounds and thriving ecosystems, have been destroyed. In 2018 the 'hypoxic' area of the Gulf of Mexico, caused by algal blooms encouraged by nitrate pollution in water drained from farms along the Mississippi river, covered 2,700 square miles[13]. Acidification by greater absorbtion of $CO_2$ by warmer water is having a dramatic effect on ocean dwellers such as crustaceans and corals, which require more alkaline conditions to make and retain their shells and exoskeletons. Since crustacea form the base of many marine food chains the consequent effect on the population of other animals which feed on them is potentially disastrous. As if these environmental problems were not enough (and I have made no mention of very real concerns over plastic and other pollutants in our oceans and freshwater), the fishing industry, for many years has plundered the oceans with little regard for sustainability. Part of the reason is the dearth of useful data on fish stock levels and fishing catches to back up effective regulation. Many fish move from place to place, making it difficult to estimate their true abundance. In areas where fishing quotas are set, using what data is available, they are often set at levels which scientists say are unsustainable. In many countries the extraordinary influence of the fishing industry causes governments to fudge effective regulation. In Europe the fishing industry accounts for about 0.1% of GDP, and even in regions most reliant on fishing, such as the Scottish Highlands or Spanish

Galicia, the proportion is little more than 2%[14]. Statistics collected by EU member States are inadequate for purpose[15]. They do not identify where fish are taken and some understate the capacity in their fleets. The EU Commission in its reports to the EU Parliament and Council downplays problems and does not include action plans.

Most ecologists and fisheries scientists agree on the problems[16]. The future of sustainable fisheries depends on less fishing, lower exploitation rates, reduced by-catch and destructive fishing methods, much more spatial management of fisheries and a significant expansion of marine ecosystem protection zones. Unfortunately the debate continues endlessly on how to achieve these aims in practice. Meanwhile, as with agriculture, techniques of industrial fishing continue to improve efficiency within the industry by 2% to 3% per year[17]. Within national coastal boundaries a level of surveillance and control can be exercised, but the open ocean beyond effectively belongs to no-one, and suffers from the same 'tragedy of the commons' that affects all those assets vital to the existence of every-one, yet owned by no-one. Even within national fishing zones many countries are unable or unwilling to police what fishing goes on. I have witnessed industrial fishing by boats from South East Asia and Europe on the Western coast of Southern India, decimating fish stocks and tipping the small indigenous fishing industry into terminal decline. It is a widespread occurrence and some estimates suggest that as local fish stocks decline the incidence of malnutrition amongst poorer communities will rise substantially[18]. More than two thirds of boats involved in illegal or unregulated fishing sail under the flag of a tax haven, despite only 4% of fishing boats overall being registered to such territories[19]. Nearly one third of all monitored fish stocks are considered to be overfished, having risen from 10% in 1974, and nearly 60% of fisheries are reckoned to be fully exploited[20]. This tale of woe coincides with a rise in world demand for fish, not simply as a result of increasing population but also because fish is generally considered a more healthy option than red meat by wealthier consumers.

Aquaculture (fish farming) worldwide has expanded enormously from 20 million tonnes in 1950 to 156.2mt in 2012, with per capita consumption of fish going from 9.9kg in 1960 to 20.2kg in 2015[21]. Most of the increase in consumption has been met by expansion of both ocean and inland freshwater aquaculture, accounting for more than half of the total human consumption of fish since 2013. Capture fisheries reached a peak of production in the 1980's and catches have levelled off since because of depletion of fishery resources. China is by far the biggest capture fishery country, almost twice as big as the next biggest, Peru, followed by Indonesia and the USA. China is also the biggest fish farming nation by far, followed by other South East Asian countries. Further expansion of fish farming is forecast to service both a growing market in developed countries and to provide a significant proportion of the protein intake of people in poorer countries. In parts of West Africa and SE Asia more than half of the protein consumed is in the form of fish[22]. An OECD/FAO 2013 prediction expected world aquaculture to expand by 35% by 2022, slightly below previous growth rates but faster than any other food producing sector.

To some extent intensively farmed fish suffer the same 'bad press' as intensively managed livestock in the eyes of many discerning consumers in developed countries. This is reflected in their preference for wild species and a willingness to pay more for them. As in other forms of intensive production, the risk of disease increases with density of stocking. The market for 'environmentally friendly' products is a reaction against destruction of the environment caused by many fish farms, including their detrimental effect on biodiversity and wild ecosystems, and their wide-spread use of fishmeal from ocean fishing as food for farmed fish. In the tropics there are places where protective mangrove swamps have been uprooted to provide space for fish farms, thereby reducing biodiversity and exposing the mainland to storm damage. Demand for fishmeal by the aquaculture sector grew from virtually nothing to utilising more than half of total production in only 20 years. Fortunately more sustainable alternatives are now being developed from vegetable protein and animal by products. More frequent El Nino weather fluctuations have impacted production from anchovy fisheries in the Pacific, from which much of the world's fishmeal is derived, bringing the price of alternatives to comparable levels.

Climate change and increased weather variability have already increased the uncertainty of supply of fish from both capture fisheries and aquaculture[23]. Predictions are for a large scale redistribution of global catch potential, increasing 30-70% in high latitude regions and decreasing by up to 40% in the tropics. This has severe implications for poor countries, exacerbated by increasing demand from wealthier ones. World production of farmed food fish increasingly relies on inland aquaculture, mainly in freshwater. In 2016 this accounted for 64.2% of farmed fish production, with China producing more than the rest of the world put together in every year since 1991[24]. Likely further expansion there risks further environmental degradation and pollution in a country where water and land resources have already been seriously compromised in the race to grow the Chinese economy.

# Chapter 13

# Problems and Solutions 2?

'Common sense is not so common',

*Voltaire*

In 1950 Sub Saharan Africans represented 10% of world population, and white Europeans or their descendants, about 30%. By the end of the 21st century these figures are likely to be 25% and 10% respectively[1]. In countries with hugely expanding populations, such as Nigeria, there is already severe poverty, deprivation and lack of employment opportunities. Where there is poor provision of education and social welfare systems poorer families tend to rear more children as a form of insurance for their old age. Smaller family size correlates to a number of social factors[2], including income level, urbanisation and, most importantly, education (especially of females), so that projections for future populations are inevitably hedged about by considerable uncertainty. The 2018 UN projection[3] for global population in 2100 therefore spanned a wide range, between 9.6 billion and 13.2 billion. Nevertheless, even the low end of this range implies very significant growth from the current (2018) 7.7 billion people.

It is evident that economic development of the poorer nations is urgent in order to prevent catastrophic poverty and to stem the tide of migration from these countries to wealthier, more secure parts of the world. Yet in these wealthier countries the level of serious political debate about economic migration and international aid to assist developing countries is notable by its absence. Instead, increasing hysteria over inward migration reflects itself in rising nationalism in many countries. Such attitudes take no account of the fast approaching demographic time-bomb within many of these self same nations. Falling fertility rates and increasing lifespans mean that a smaller proportion of working age people are left to drive economic progress and support an increasingly expensive older generation.

Across all OECD countries in 1970 the total fertility rate (number of children per female) was 2.7. A rate of 2.1 is needed to maintain a stable population because not every child that is born will go on to have children of its own. By 2018 average fertility was 1.7 children per female, well below the replacement rate. In South Korea, the 1970 figure of 4.5 had dropped by 2018 to 1.2, and in China, where a one-child policy was enforced between 1979 and 2015, from 5.6 to 1.6. Despite the removal of the one-child policy many, particularly urban Chinese continue not to have second children, citing high living costs, lack of affordable childcare and later marriage[4].

Wide disparities in population growth in different areas of the world are not mirrored exactly by patterns of food demand. Economic growth and the rise of the global middle class , most notably in China, has disproportionately skewed higher demand for meat and dairy products. As we have seen this has implications for agriculture and for the environment not just in the countries concerned, but across the world. It is, for example, one of the most important causes of environmental degradation in South America where rainforest and wilderness are being destroyed for cattle raising and for the production of soyabean for export as animal feed. And the rising overall demand for food globally is the stimulus for greater intensity of production and increased trade in food and agricultural commodities.

The 2019 Lancet *EAT Commission Report*[5] highlights '*the danger of commercial vested interest, lack of political leadership and insufficient societal demand for change*' in shifting diets toward more healthy options. The result is … '*rising rates of obesity, greenhouse gas emissions and stagnating rates of under-nutrition*'. It calls for international action to agree a '*global treaty to limit the political influence of 'Big Food', modelled on the global conventions on tobacco and climate change*'. Were such a treaty to be established and be effective in changing widespread attitudes to food it would undoubtedly reduce the pressures of current food systems on land and water use globally, and be a major boost to efforts to contain the damage we collectively do to ecosystems, as well as benefiting human health. It would also help, to some degree, the wider global effort needed to combat climate change. International cooperation between environmentalists and the medical profession should carry sufficient authority to influence consumers against overconsumption of high nutrient density foodstuffs which are implicated in rising rates of heart disease, obesity, diabetes and dietary related cancers. Although many of these conditions are related to excessive refined carbohydrate consumption and insufficient physical activity, any reduction in meat consumption (or, at least a reduction in the rate of increase in consumption) on a world scale, would be welcomed by conservationists. Using less of the earths surface to grow crops directly or indirectly for meat production allows more to be available for wildlife and for the provision of the ecosystem services so vital for a healthy planet. On a global scale greater afforestation and reduced usage of artificial fertiliser and pesticides would be beneficial, subject to the overriding need to feed everyone sufficiently well.

Within the agricultural industry there are those who advocate the need for technical progress in raising productivity whilst improving the environmental credentials of the industry, but believe that the land no longer required for food would be better used to grow crops for fuel or industrial substrate to replace fossil fuels supplies. I do not propose here to examine the technical arguments for or against this proposal, save to comment that there may also be a social argument for governments to support it. In chapter 10 I noted the problems that face many farmers in finding viable alternative strategies in order to continue their businesses. Growing biofuels might help close that gap, enabling some farmers, who might otherwise be driven out of business, to survive.

Simple solutions are rarely possible in a complex system like agriculture. Take meat production as an example. A report prepared for the January 2019 World Economic Forum in Davos by the International Livestock Research Institute (ILRI) for their 'Meat the Future' series of briefings looks at options in developing economies[6]. The projected demand for livestock derived food in Africa (2010-30) is for an increase in volume of 80%. But this demand is not driven by over-consumption, because the starting point is a consumption level per capita of one sixth the average level of OECD countries. Rather, the rise in demand is due to fast growing populations consuming the same amount or less per head. By contrast, in those Asian nations where populations are beginning to stabilise, but where incomes are rising, demand for meat is rising as people can afford to consume more. Roughly one third of world population consumes an adequate well balanced diet, one third is overfed and suffers from overweight or obesity and one third is underfed or malnourished[7]. Those in the last category, whose current access to meat or dairy products is severely limited, will require a very different policy to enhance their diets compared with people in the other categories.

There are many different reasons for keeping livestock. In some societies the reason may be cultural or religious (such as sacred cows in India). In others, apart from providing employment and income, livestock may be the most convenient 'savings bank', a source of wealth. How livestock are owned and managed also varies enormously, including individual or cooperative ownership to commercial company. Systems may vary from pastoral common land grazing to intensive feedlot. Different systems of management may be harmful to the local environment or vital to the nutrient cycle of producing food crops. So it is clear that solutions primarily need to reflect local needs, whilst having due regard to global priorities. Where these two objectives collide, ideally it is the job of government to find appropriate compromise solutions which garner international support and understanding.

In countries where currently excessive consumption of meat per capita is expected to decline, livestock farmers may find themselves in a difficult position. Their governments may decline to support an industry where demand is falling. Trade liberalisation would dictate that if these countries can produce at lower cost, their surpluses should find ready export markets. But as I have noted, agriculture and food is notorious for the range and number of restrictive trade agreements, levies and non-trade barriers raised to protect domestic production, maintain quality, health and welfare standards, and help to maintain a strategically and socially important sector of the economy. In chapter 6 I referred to the suggestion by Professor Alan Buckwell[8] that global population growth may be used as a convenient shorthand to justify protection of EU agriculture despite the decline of domestic markets. Wealthy countries with powerful agri-food interests, such as the USA, Japan and countries in the EU have traditionally subsidised and protected their agricultural sectors to the detriment of poorer countries. Efforts to liberalise trade in agricultural products have been slower and much less successful than with many industrial goods and unilateral action by an individual country can be counterproductive, leading to the decimation of all or part of its own farming industry or unfairly skewing the competitive balance against farms in other countries.

Other pressures within countries, particularly in Europe, target what are seen as over intensive forms of animal production. Largely led by animal welfare groups they raise concerns over what are seen as 'cruel' systems of confinement and slaughtering methods. So called 'factory' farms are especially targeted with the somewhat irrational view that smaller farms are somehow better at managing livestock than larger farms. Paradoxically it is often the larger and more economically viable farms which can afford to invest in technical innovations and staff training and education which may benefit the animals and the environment, whilst making food more available to consumers at a reasonable price. All meat producers of whatever size of business face a rising challenge from non-meat meat substitutes, some of which may also have greater environmental and health promoting credentials. This type of competition is likely to increase and will present a further challenge to the livelihood of many livestock farmers. American consultancy AT Kearney predicts that by 2040 only 40% of meat or meat substitute consumption will come from conventional sources[9].

In the crop production sector, technological advances are necessary to address increasing environmental problems, for raising output, increasing yield and reducing income volatility, as well as improving nutritional values. I noted in chapter 6 the growing public and political pressure on many of the technologies which drove the green revolution of the 1970's. In some countries this pressure also extends to more modern technologies such as gene editing, which potentially offer faster resolution to major problems from resistance of weeds and disease pathogens to current methods of control, the need to reduce fertiliser use and to improve crop quality, yield and reliability. Not far from my home, in the world renowned John Innes Institute, scientists are studying the mechanism by which some plants, in symbiosis with bacteria, are able to fix atmospheric nitrogen. 45% of protein in the human diet comes from plants grown using artificial nitrogen fertiliser[10], but applications already exceed planetary boundaries and are unsustainable in the long term. Even if all the processes by which legumes currently fix nitrogen are discovered, the transference of this ability to other classes of crop plant by genetic manipulation would currently be denied by EU legislation, blocking the prospect of hugely benign environmental improvement. It would similarly block the practical application of work currently underway at the University of Illinois[11],where a more efficient form of photosynthesis found in some bacteria and algae has been shown experimentally to improve the productivity of modified crop plants by up to 40%.

Arguments still go on between environmentalists and food producers over which type of farming is more beneficial to nature – land 'sparing' (intensive production on a smaller area of land) or land 'sharing' (low intensity agriculture shared with some conservation practices, but using more land globally for the equivalent amount of food production). Many academics have concluded that land 'sparing', now called 'sustainable intensification', is better[12,13]. Were there to be a drop in demand for meat and dairy products as a result of a massive global dietary shift change, the debate would clearly arise once more. But that, in the foreseeable future seems unlikely. Shifts will be gradual at best, and while organic principles contain much of interest within sustainable intensification practice, the reactionary approach to almost all modern technology taken by some organic pundits and consumer pressure groups, is not helpful in addressing many issues of world food sustainability.

The foregoing examples illustrate the severe headwinds any comprehensive set of solutions must face on the way to being accepted both within societies and between nations. As I indicated at the very beginning of this book, improved stewardship of the earths resources is vitally important. The extent to which the worldwide agriculture and food sector has damaged its own 'factory floor' – the soil – is tragic. Similarly, human exploitation of precious water supplies takes little account of longer term needs, and threatens the livelihood of future generations in many parts of the world. Yet most farmers are not by nature deliberate 'asset strippers', but they often face multiple pressures which encourage them to farm for today rather than for tomorrow.

When I first started in farming everything seemed much simpler. The clear objective was to produce as much as possible and to do it as efficiently as possible. There were no worries about environmental destruction. Indeed government subsidised me generously to tear out hedgerows, make fields bigger to accommodate larger machinery, drain wet areas and lay concrete roads around the farm. It provided at no cost to me, a band of advisers able to help plan cropping programmes, advise on new technologies and marketing of my produce. It helped me be so successful that, within a few years, that same government offered me grants to put hedges back again and to stop growing crops on a portion of my land. Perverse incentives from well meaning governments have certainly encouraged farmers to do things they might not otherwise have done. At the same time, in the UK, intense pressure on farmers to produce cheap food for the masses was looked on with favour by government and largely actioned through international competition and a powerful retail sector driving down prices and ensuring profit margins were generally low. So state subsidies to maintain farmer incomes became a way of life. Those same margin pressures that necessitated subsidies stimulated innovation, but also intensification. And, it must be said that most farmers welcomed new technology which often made work less physically demanding. Most were ignorant through the 70's and 80's of the damage they were causing to the environment, and even today many are in denial over the extent to which farming is responsible for declining numbers of farmland birds, insects and wild species of plants. But of course a similar state of denial exists in the wider population over climate change, environmental degradation and unhealthy lifestyles.

Today farmers face a dilemma. How should they plan for the future when the objectives are so diverse and unclear compared with the 1970's when I began farming? In the affluent West we produce too much food, arguably at prices which are too low, encouraging unsustainable and unacceptable practices. Getting off that treadmill is difficult, and those who have opted instead for 'niche' production at higher prices and lower intensity only survive so long as prices remain high. In other words, so long as not too many others follow their example and flood the market. High prices are unaffordable for less well off consumers, so governments inevitably favour low food prices and ample supply, coupled with special payments to keep farmers in business, which increasingly take the form of payments for environmental measures of various kinds.

I have already outlined the health arguments for reducing individual food consumption, particularly of foods containing excess sugar, and red meats. Should such change come about the demand for some products in these countries will fall, and some new opportunities will arise for healthier products such as fruit and vegetables. But for farmers it won't be a simple swap of one enterprise for another. Many farmers will not find viable alternatives; their land may not be suitable, they may require more capital or labour than is available, their likely returns may be too volatile, or the new products may be grown more cheaply elsewhere. And their options will be further constrained by environmental regulation and what the public consider to be acceptable practice. One response to this dilemma is to exploit export markets for surplus produce. This is already a reality, for instance, as a means of balancing supply and demand for the various cuts of pigmeat. Processors in the UK and Europe export many of the cuts less popular on the home markets to the Far East, where they are valued. Europe exports bacon to the UK market whilst the UK exports its surplus pork legs to Europe. Trade between countries in agricultural commodities and food is generally helpful to economic growth and development, but some growth has been at too high an environmental cost. Less common than it was is the practice of countries with surplus production, particularly the USA, subsidising exports to developing countries in order to support domestic prices. Trade restrictions generally prevent similar traffic in the opposite direction, but because of weak governance in many developing countries there are few trade barriers to prevent such produce 'dumping' undermining the already precarious livelihoods of their own farming sectors.

Farmers in developing countries often face a set of problems different to those in rich countries, although they stem from the same requirement to maintain an adequate lifestyle. With increasing populations, lack of demand for the food is not the problem. Instead, the question is how to meet that demand as much as possible from domestic resources. The starting point is often numerous smallholdings on poor land, with little access to capital or even basic technology. Sources of advice may be hard to find and lack of adequate infrastructure such as roads, storage facilities or functioning markets may hamper business development and increase the likelihood of food wastage. Increasing risk of drought or flood exacerbates income volatility and even threatens survival. Farmers may have poor security of tenure and little incentive to plan for anything other than the short-term.

Such brief examples illustrate the difficulties faced by farmers across the world when so many unpredictable external factors beyond their control have such critical potential to affect their lives and livelihoods. They are not in control of their own futures to the extent that I thought I was as a farmer starting out just a few years before. What happens in international trade talks and agreements? What action is taken to change consumer eating habits, both nationally and internationally? What industrial processes or innovative research might disrupt and force system change on farms? What environmental restraints are imposed on farming and the food industry? All these issues, as yet unresolved, will substantially affect the decisions that individual farmers have to take. Theirs is a long term business which needs, for its survival, long term assurance and policy continuity. Answers to these questions are currently lacking, certainly at the international level, and within most countries they are only partially addressed, and usually in an uncoordinated fashion.

With all this uncertainty, there remains 'the elephant in the room' of climate change. The urgency and scope of actions to address this, taken across the every economy in the world will heavily impinge on all the other issues I have mentioned. Some of the wider changes needed in society and government is what I turn to next.

# Chapter 14

# Problems and Solutions 3?

'In the field of world policy I would dedicate this nation to the policy of the good neighbour'.

*Franklin D. Roosevelt, Inaugural address as US President, 1933*

The clock is ticking on the actions that can be taken to slow climate change. Climate scientists are becoming ever more strident in their warnings, and more certain of the damage that will be done to the environment as increasing data from current events confirms the trends shown in their climate prediction models. The IPCC 2018 special report on the need to hold global average warming to 1.5°C above pre-industrial levels clearly demonstrated the significant benefits that achieving this lower target would imply for natural systems and for poorer regions of the world, especially the tropics. But that report came with a warning that the remaining carbon budget (the amount of $CO_2$ or equivalent that can be safely released into the atmosphere in order to keep below the 1.5°C threshold) is very small. That implies that decarbonisation of the global economy needs to proceed at an unprecedented rate, and that even if this can be achieved, untested techniques such as carbon capture and storage (CCS) will be needed, at scale, in order to improve the chances of meeting the target. The fact that the carbon budget is already very small heightens the importance of measures to reduce greenhouse gas emissions (GHG's) from the agriculture and food sectors. Without significant reductions here there will be little chance of the overall target being met. Even though the major agricultural GHG's, methane and nitrous oxide, are less long lasting than $CO^2$ in the atmosphere, while they continue to be produced they affect the carbon budget[1].

In December 2018, French President Emmanuel Macron was forced by public demonstrations to reverse a planned tax increase introduced to curb greenhouse gas emissions from diesel fuel[2]. In the US, Canada, Australia and elsewhere, leaders found their efforts to tax emissions, through carbon pricing or other methods, ran into fierce opposition from rank and file voters as well as from well financed industry lobbies. In Australia in 2019 voters re-elected a climate sceptic government which supports further exploitation of coal reserves despite evident climate changes which seriously threaten the future economy of the country. To make carbon taxation more electorally palatable, in Canada Prime Minister Justin Trudeau unveiled a $C10/ton carbon tax in 2018, rising to $C50 by 2022, from which roughly 90% of revenue will be repaid to consumers in the form of climate action incentive payments. Because of progressive tax rates, about 70% of Canadians will get back more than they paid – even more if they choose to be more energy efficient. Even so, there is considerable opposition from several of the Canadian provinces to accept the plan, which was designed to allow Canada to meet its commitment under the Paris agreement to bring down 2005 $CO_2$ levels 30% by 2030.

Only in a few places have carbon taxes been successfully adopted to date, including Chile, Spain, Ukraine, Ireland and the Scandinavian countries. In the UK electricity generation from renewable sources, such as wind and solar, is supported by minimum price guarantees from Government, which raises the price charged to domestic consumers and to industry. This has met with stiff opposition, particularly from power hungry industries, such as steelmaking, which claim that the extra costs make it difficult for them to compete internationally.

To stimulate the actions needed across the global economy, increasing numbers of scientists and others, such as the interim President of the World Bank[3], call for realistic taxation of carbon to encourage a faster transition to a 'greener' future. Such taxes have been used for several years in the EU and elsewhere, but only in certain sectors of the economy, and never at levels which were truly effective. Only 20% of global emissions are currently charged a carbon tax[4], and only 1% face a price as high as $40 per tonne of $CO^2$. To achieve the 1.5°C degree pathway, Prof. Simon Dietz[5] suggests an across the board price of $100 per tonne of $CO_2$, rising year by year. Nothing remotely as high as this figure has yet been levied in any country. As I said in chapter 11 this would significantly increase the price of food and pose the threat of hunger and malnutrition to many people, especially in poorer countries.

Some Democratic politicians in the USA now propose a 'New Green Deal[6]', which, instead of imposing high carbon taxes relies on stimulating public acceptance through massive public sector investment on the lines of the Roosevelt 'New Deal' of the 1930's. It seems unlikely that such an idea will generate sufficient traction in a country so wedded to the concept of 'small government', and most other countries would be unable to emulate the level of deficit budgeting that would be required. It nevertheless raises the question of how to persuade people that costly change is necessary, either funded directly through increased prices or indirectly through government spending, ultimately financed by taxation.

It is clear that democratically elected politicians do not feel they have the power needed to fulfil their long-term responsibilities. To effect change, even the most popular and competent ones must work within a lawful framework and what might be termed 'establishment opinion'. And as events in different countries in the last few years have shown, people do not like paying more than token amounts for green policies. As a result, where measures are introduced by governments they tend to be very selective, sometimes at lower levels than optimal to achieve target outcomes. The 'polluter pays' principle is widely cited, but much less frequently applied to control corporate excess, particularly where consumers perceive immediate connection between extra costs on business and the price they pay for goods and services.

Where regulation is applied compliance is often costly for businesses. In my younger days I regularly lobbied government to allow my industry (pig production) to develop voluntary methods to address problem areas, in order to ensure that extra costs were minimised and actions required were practical for producers to apply. One example was a scheme to reduce the overuse of antibiotics by asking producers to enter their herd usage on a central database, which in turn provided the peer pressure to drive down unnecessary consumption. That system is working effectively today. In some situations, however, voluntary measures prove ineffective or are too slow to work. The Chief Medical Officer of England is on record for criticising food companies for insufficient efforts taken to reduce sugar and salt content in items such as biscuits, cakes and chocolate[7]. Her comments followed reports that childhood obesity in England in 2018 was four times higher than in 1990, and that by the age of ten the average child has consumed the whole sugar allowance it needs to develop into a healthy adult. Industry has been asked to voluntarily cut sugar and salt in their products by 5% per annum, but so far has only managed 2%. By contrast, following the imposition of a fizzy drinks tax, sugar levels in affected products fell by an average of 11%.

People resent being told what to eat or drink by a 'nanny state', particularly when it costs them more. Research by Dr. Marco Springmann of the Oxford Martin School[8] suggested that red meat would need to be 20% more expensive, and processed meat, such as bacon would need to double in price in order to fund 70% of the health costs associated with their consumption. Bringing about change of this order would be unpopular and probably take a long time. It would require what the Global Food Security programme calls a 'food systems approach' – implying multidisciplinary cooperation and understanding in driving forward an agreed long-term strategy to achieve the desired outcomes. This strategy might include public procurement policies, minimum standards for health and sustainability, better labelling and integration of data down the food chain, rebalancing of subsidies from energy rich to nutrient rich crops, true cost accounting and focussing on efficiency in achieving healthy people fed per unit of input rather than yield per unit input[9]. It follows that this approach demands policy coherence across agriculture, nutrition, health, trade and the environment. And there lies a tremendous challenge to current practices.

For some years I was a non-executive Director on a local health Board, part of the UK National Health Service. Despite the best intentions of managers and staff, poor internal and external communications, lack of understanding of local needs by more senior levels of management and oppressive levels of bureaucracy stood in the way of effective integration of services. It taught me a lesson in how difficult it is in practice to achieve 'joined-up' solutions to complex problems. Paul Johnson, director of the Institute for Fiscal Studies on a similar theme[10], wrote about the short term focus of too many policymakers and the shocking ignorance of many of them about advances in research. He suggested, '*Too many researchers are dismissive of the needs of government and equally ignorant of the policy making process. As a result the two communities are far less than the potential sum of their parts*'. He goes on to criticise the lack of openness within government and the waste of resources resulting from under-use and inadequate analysis of data held in separate databases. I am reminded of the quotation attributed to John Stuart Mill, the 19th century political economist and civil servant, '*He who only knows his own side of the case knows little of that*'.

The fault does not lie only with government. I have referred at various points in the text to the clash of corporate interests with community good. A 'softer' kind of capitalism which takes community interest into account is slowly spreading across the corporate world, but that goes nowhere near far enough to meet the level of challenge outlined in this book. Globalisation has brought more economic progress to more people than anything else in history, but it has also exacerbated risk. What may be rational behaviour for individuals or corporations is increasingly irrational for society as a whole. Economic growth has come at the expense of the environment we all enjoy, but nature is not capable of responding to market signals. It does not become more productive when the prices of its products rise, and in consequence, increased choice for humans has resulted in over exploitation of natural systems. As I argued in chapter 11 we are in dire need of a practical economic system which is able to take proper account both of the 'commons', which are shared by all but belong to no-one, and of the 'external' costs borne by society as a whole for the indulgence of individuals, such as the costs of healthcare caused by bad diets and poor lifestyles.

Despite all the increasingly strident warnings about climate change, global demand for oil is still rising. Exxon Mobil, the biggest of the oil majors, plans to pump 25% more oil and gas in 2025 than in 2019[11], and predicts that global oil and gas demand will increase by 13% by 2030. At the IPPC meeting in Katowice (2018) the USA joined Saudi Arabia, Kuwait and Russia in blocking a proposal to embrace formally the UN study which details the planetary consequences of of $1.5^0$C of warming against the $2^0$C target agreed in Paris in 2015. And the Washington Post recorded[12] that US $CO_2$ emissions rose by 3.4% in 2018 alongside rises from China and India, resulting in total global emissions reaching a record high. These are examples of national and corporate self interest taking precedence over rational global policy. Climate change is a classic 'free-rider' problem. GHG emissions occur locally, but have global effects. The world would benefit enormously if all countries reduced their emissions, but no individual country will benefit much by reducing its own emissions unilaterally.

The power of multinational corporations to change the agri-food sector was described in chapter 10. Globalisation has vastly increased the volume of agricultural commodity and food trading and the spread of 'western style' diets across the world. It has certainly contributed to spreading economic well being but it has also spread the obesity epidemic and diet associated health problems, as well as stimulating greater environmental exploitation and damage. Together with multinationals in other economic sectors they have effectively reduced the space for the sovereignty of national governments to control their own affairs. That sovereignty is also reduced by the need for countries to come together to agree common rules and standards for trade in goods, services and capital. In itself this is a good thing, offering a route for further international cooperation, but globalisation and the inequalities it has produced within economies is suffering from a nationalistic backlash in many countries. This threatens the likelihood of international cooperation to deal with global challenges.

So there are real barriers to better cooperation from consumers unwilling to look beyond their immediate concerns, from businesses with insufficient responsibility for the public good, and from governments unable or unwilling to take principled but potentially unpopular actions both nationally and internationally. But the primary objective of this book is to outline the urgent need to create a broad understanding across multiple sectors and interests as the basis for prioritising long term goals which properly and comprehensively address the challenges which face us all. It is time for a new generation of informed generalists and polymaths to take control of our decision making. It is not a time for tribalism, closed minds, single issue extremism or an unwillingness to cooperate and compromise.

During the course of researching and writing this book, over a long period (2013-19) it has been heartening to observe a number of influential bodies arriving at similar conclusions. Initially those calling for action on climate change virtually ignored the agri-food sector and its contribution to the problem and to its potential for helping to alleviate it. The looming world food problem used to be seen through a separate lens, essentially as a crisis to be confronted by improving farmers technical efficiency and driving up yields through scientific innovation, whilst in parallel seeking to reduce the environmental footprint of the sector. Diet and health were in a separate box, to be dealt with through a different set of measures, rather than as problems indissolubly linked with changing agricultural systems and benefitting ecosystems. Only in the last year or two have reports been published demanding coordination of policies – as the UK Global Food Security programme calls it, a '*food systems approach*'[13]. This is mirrored by similar objectives internationally, described in the 2019 Lancet EAT Commission Report[14] calling for the establishment of an international treaty to agree on holistic global solutions.

From the perspective of an individual farmer the prospect of some certainty of direction for his or her business or livelihood is appealing, even though it is likely to necessitate considerable change to current practices. Farming is nothing if not resilient, if given the time, encouragement and steadfastness of purpose from government, business and consumers, to deliver what is required by society as a whole.

This would seem to be a natural place to draw this book to a conclusion. I have put forward what I hope are balanced arguments based on reason, science, practical politics and human psychology. I have alluded to the absence of reason in some human reactions to the crises that society face – in particular, the tendency to self interest and unwillingness to accept, or even try to understand different viewpoints. I am already beyond my three score years and ten so I have written about many things I will not live to see come to fruition. Paradoxically that makes me feel it all the more necessary to try to influence for the better, the kind of future that my descendants will face. There is much more to life than material well being. There is also an innate need in all of us to feel that we have acted responsibly. I shall end, therefore with a short chapter I entitle 'morality'.

# Chapter 15
# Morality

'We don't do God'

*Alistair Campbell, Communication Director to PM Tony Blair*

I began, in the foreword to this book, by describing the wisdom of ancient civilisations in Australia and North America. Their cultures recognised something beyond pure self interest; an awareness of something greater than themselves; a respect for the environment around them, which provided for all their needs as long as they took proper care of it. For both cultures, 'ownership' of their world was a foreign concept – they could not take any part of their world with them when they died, but whilst they lived they could be good stewards over it, to ensure that succeeding generations could enjoy the bounty they had received. We have no reason to suppose these civilisations were less content with their lot than the present generation. Indeed, though most modern societies enjoy vastly better material living standards and security there are evidently increasing levels of dissatisfaction with current economic, social and political conditions. So many of the gains humanity has made in the last few centuries can be attributed to the advance of science and of reason, but this same advance may also be eroding what, for centuries provided a fundamental source of security, a purpose for living, a faith or a creed in something unknowable, but infinitely bigger than ourselves.

The search for a 'purpose' can sometimes manifest itself in extremist ideologies – a negation of all that our forefathers taught but it can also be seen in many religious teachings and in widely held concerns for universal human rights and values. The Sustainable Development Goals, 2015 (SDG's), agreed by the United Nations demonstrate a general underlying concensus for working together as one human species toward better stewardship of our world, our environment and all that lives within it. They are a recognition that ideals and human values should be as much a part of politics as self interest.

We often think of Prime Minister, Margaret Thatcher as one of the high priests of exploitative capitalism, but in a speech to the UN General Assembly on 8th November 1989[1] she said, *'We should always remember that free markets are a means to an end. They would defeat their object, if, by their output they did more damage to the quality of life ... than the well being they achieve through the production of goods and services'.* In saying this she was reflecting the views of the father of modern economic theory, Adam Smith, who was very clear in his seminal work *'The Wealth of Nations'* that *'the wise and virtuous man is always willing that his own private interest should be sacrificed to the public interest*[2].

It is all too easy to focus solely on the potential of capitalism for material enrichment and to foster a culture where material progress becomes the 'purpose'. Karl Marx postulated that such exploitative capitalism was bound to destroy itself once the potential for growth had been exhausted. What he did not foresee was the deformed creature that communism itself would become, nor the ability of capitalism to keep on reinventing itself. Such a reinvention is urgently needed now, with the prospect of declining long term economic growth constrained by over exploitation of earth's resources and the need to recognise new social, cultural and ethical norms as a basis for political economy. Economics is so much more than money, which is simply a means of converting multiple perceived values into a single and easily understood system of transferable assets.

There is a case to be made for capitalism because it encourages independence, creativity, ambition and hard work. In an interview with the Times[3], UK Chancellor, Philip Hammond addressed the real concerns of many young people; *'A key part of convincing the next generation that we have a coherent strategy for managing our economy is going to be demonstrating that a market based economic system is compatible with environmental responsibility'.* There is much to do if these words are to be translated into practice. Above all it is vital to gain international agreement and cooperation. It is simply not practical for a single country to take action unilaterally. Nor is it possible without the active support of the business community, where powerful vested interests so often stand in the way of political change. In medieval times the concept of a company was of a family business, comprising people who 'took bread' together, (hence *cum panis* which became *company*). Within such a close knit group the simple pursuit of profit at the expense of all other consideration would have been unlikely. The motivations for business would surely have been to satisfy a range of needs and wishes of the family group. For modern corporations their 'family' must be society as a whole.

That human family now faces an intense period of change, making it imperative that the scope and complexity of challenges is more widely understood. Good decisions are unlikely to be made if we cannot clearly discern the consequences, or if the complexity of the situation increases faster than the understanding. That makes current challenges problematic – people tend to resist the speed of change if they cannot understand the reason for it. Willingness to change is weakened by lack of trust in those who are leading. In western societies in particular, the diminishing influence of traditional faiths and weakening of ethical and moral standards in society contributes to greater unwillingness to be 'good neighbours' today and 'good stewards' for future generations.

I draw encouragement chiefly from the attitudes of the younger generation, many of whom recognise that the problems of the future are the responsibility of the present generation to address. I despair of many in my own older generation, whose reaction to learning more about the looming problems described in this book is all too often to shrug their shoulders and do nothing. More than he knew at the time, Alistair Campbell reflected the sorry moral state of the nation when he made the comment which heads this chapter.

In my many years of service on committees and public bodies of various kinds I have learned that apathy is pernicious. Someone willing to take a stand and be prepared to put thought and effort into achieving a goal is disproportionately likely to achieve that goal. Activity achieves results, but my argument in this book is not for activity for narrow ends, but to achieve widespread and broad understanding which then leads on to concerted action. This is a time for polymaths; specifically for polymaths who recognise, as did President Eisenhower (see also ch. 10) '*that farming looks mighty easy when your plough is a pencil and you're 1000 miles from the cornfield*'. It is a time for generalists who are prepared to look beyond narrowly defined horizons whilst others bear the load, and who do not sit back but get involved. It is a time for many more of us to become good stewards.

# References

**Introduction**

1  Bryson, Bill: *At Home: a short history of private life*, ISBN 978-0-385-66163-8 (2010)

**Foreword**

1  IPBES 2019 *Global Assessment Report on Biodiversity and Ecosystem Services*, www.ipbes.net

2  King, Mervyn: *The End of Alchemy; Money, Banking and the future of the Global Economy*, ISBN 978-1-4087-0610-7 (2016)

3  Boyd, A., Swinburn et al: *The Global Syndemic of Obesity, Undernutrition and Climate Change: The Lancet Commission Report;* https:thelancet.com/journals/lancet/article/PIIS0140-6736(18)32822-8/fulltext

**Chapter 1 Population**

1  Erhlich, Paul, R. *The Population Bomb* (1968) ISBN 978-0-345-02139-7

2  UK Government Office for Science: *Foresight Project on Global Food and Farming Futures: Synthesis Report C1: trends in food demand and production;* First published January 2011

3  Gerland, P. Et al: *World population stabilization unlikely this centu*ry; Science, **346**, issue 6206, pp. 234-237: 10th October 2014: DOI 10-1126/science.1257469

4  The Royal Society Policy Centre Report 01/12: *People and the Planet:* April 2012 DES 2470: ISBN 978-0-85403-955-5

5  United Nations Department of Economic and Social Affairs: *World population prospects; the 2017 revision:* https//www.un.org.development/.../world-population-prospects-the-2017-revision.html

6  *Ibid. ref.* 2

7  *Ibid.* ref. 5

8  *Now for the Long Term: The Report of the Oxford Martin Commission for Future Generations: October 2013:* https//www.oxfordmartin.ox.ac.uk

9  Keats, S., Wiggins, S. *Population change in the rural development world: making the transition:* March 2016, Overseas Development Institute

10 *Ibid.* ref. 2

11 World Economic Forum 2016: *The Global Risks Report 2016, 11th Edition:* https//www.wef.ch.risks2016

## Chapter 2 Climate Change

1  http://www.influencemap.org/filter/List-of-Companies-and-influencers
2  Rockstrom, J. Et al; *Planetary Boundaries: Exploring the Safe Operating Space for Humanity;* Ecology and Society, **14**, (2): 32 (online) http//www.ecologyand-society.org/vol14/iss2/art32
3  http//www.shoppervista.igd.com *shopper sentiment reports:changing food choicesin the UK*, 27/09/2013
4  http//www.newyorktimes.com/2015/02/01/business/energy-environment/climate-changes-bottom-line.html?emc=eta1&_r=1
5  The UK Committee on Climate Change, *Net Zero – The UK's contribution to stopping global warming,* 2nd May 2019, www.theccc.org.uk
6  Stern, N., *The Economics of Climate Change: The Stern Review:* Cambridge University Press (2007), ISBN 978-0-521-70080, and in lecture to Overseas Development Institute, London on 19th November 2015
7  Lawson, N., *An Apeal to Reason: a cool look at global warming:* Duckworth Overlook (2009) ISBN 100-715-638-416
8  http//www.bbc.co.uk/news/resources/idt-5aceb360-8bc3-4741-99f0-2e4f76ca02bb
9  http//www.thenational.ae/world/asia/india-food-crisis-likely: January 30th 2018
10 Berners-Lee, M., Clark, D., *The Burning Question:we can't burn half the world's oil, coal and gas, so how do we quit?* Profile Books (2013), ISBN 978-1-78125-045-7
11 IPPC 2014; Summary for Policymakers in; *Climate Change 2014: Mitigation of Climate Change Contribution of Working Group III to the Fifth Assessment Report of the Intergovernmental Panel on Climate Change;* (Edenhofer, O., et al), Cambridge University Press, Cambridge, United Kingdom and New York, NY, USA
12 Nerem, R.S., et al: *Climate-change-driven accelerated sea level rise detected in the altimeter era;* PNAS February 27th 2018, **115**, (9), *2022–2025;* http//www.doi.org/10-1073/pnas.1717312115

## Chapter 3 Climate Change and Agriculture

1  CCAFS. CGIAR Research Program on Climate Change, Agriculture and Food Security Factsheet. CGIAR Research Program on Climate Change, Agriculture and Food Security (CCAFS), Copenhagen, Denmark (2014).
2  Thornton, P., 2012, *Recalibrating Food Production in the Developing World: Global warming will change more than just the climate.* CCAFS Policy Brief no.6. CGIAR Research Program on Climate Change, Agriculture and Food Security. (CCAFS). http//www.ccafs.cgiar.org
3  Medek, D.E., Schwartz, J., Myers, S.S., *estimated effects of future atmospheric $CO_2$ concentrations on protein intake, and the risk of protein deficiency by country and region;* Environmental Health Perspectives, **125**, (8), 087002

4  Stanford News, May 1st 2014. Report of research by Lobell, D. Et al: *US corn yields are increasingly vulnerable to hot dry weather, Stanford research shows.*

5  http//www.maplecroft.com/solutions/environment-climate-change

6  Depak K. Ray, James S. Gerber, et al. *Climate variation explains a third of crop yield variability;* Nature Communications, **6**, article no.5989 (2015)

7  Zabel, F., Putzenlechner, B., Mauser, W.,(2014), *Global Agricultural Land Resources – a high resolution suitability evaluation and its perspectives until 2100 under climate change conditions;* PLoS ONE, **9**, (9): e107522 http//doi.org/10.1371/journal.pone.0107522

8  UNCTAD/DITC/TED/2012/3 United Nations Publications ISSN 1810-5432

9  CarbonBrief guest blog by Tim Benton and Bajana Bajzelj, *Food and Agriculture in the Carbon Budget and COP21 agreement;* on http//www.frcn.org.uk; food security and nutrition reference site dated 20th April 2016

10  *Ibid.* 5, Chapter 2

11  Tully, Katherine, et al. *The state of Soil Degradation in Sub-Saharan-Africa: Baseline Trajectories and solutions;* Sustainability **2015,** 7, 6523-6552; doi 10.3390/su7066523 http//www.mdpi.com/journal/sustainability ISSN 2071-1050

12  FAO's Work on Climate Change; United Nations Climate Change Conference 2015 Facts and Figures (p.8)

13  McKinsey Quarterly; *Africa's path to growth: sector by sector* (June 2010)

**Chapter 4 Water**

1  Rockstrom, J., et al; *(see ref.2, chapter 2)*

2  UN Environment Global Environment Outlook GEO6 (2019); online and from Cambridge University Press, http//www.cambridge.org/9781108707688

3  IFPRI *Global Food Policy Report 2016*, chapter 5, p.35; http//www.ifpri.org/publication/2016-global-food-policy-report

4  World Economic Forum (see ref.8, chapter 1)

5  World Bank.2016: *High and Dry: Climate Change, Water and the Economy; Executive summary:* World Bank; Washington DC; License: Creative Commons Attribution CCBY 3.OIGO http//www.worldbank.org/en/…water/…/high-and-dry-climate-change-water-and-the-economy

6  United Nations World Water Assessment Program (WWAP), 2015, *The United Nations World Water Development Report: Water for a Sustainable World;* Paris, UNESCO

7  The Water Integrity Network Association e.V. The Water Integrity Global Outlook (WIGO), 2016, (WIN), ISBN: 978-3-00-051295-7, http//www.waterintegritynetwork.net

8   As referenced by SAIN (UK-China Sustainable Agriculture Innovation Network) announcement on Chinese TV (CCTV) 4th May 2016 from the Chinese National People's Conference.

9   Jaegermayr, J., et al (2016); *Integrated crop water management might sustainably halve the global food gap;* Environmental Research Letters, **11,** 025002 (doi:10-1088/1748-9326/11/2/025002), http//iopscience.iop.org/article/10-1088/1748-9326/11/2/025002

10  McKinsey Quarterly; *Confronting South Africa's Water Challenge;* June 2010

11  Strzepek, K, Boehlert, B., 2010; *Competition for water for the food system;* Philosophical Transactions of the Royal Society, **B 365,** 2927-2940

12  Food and Climate Research Network (FCRN); Dr. Tim Hess, Cranfield University, blog post on www.fcrn.org.uk on 22nd February 2016

13  Foresight. *The Future of Food and Farming (2011), Final Project Report;* The Government Office for Science, London, (p.15)

**Chapter 5 Soil**

1   IFPRI (see ref.3, chapter 4)

2   UN Environmental Outlook (see ref.2, chapter 4)

3   IFPRI (ibid)

4   McKinsey Quarterly; *Extreme climate conditions – how Africa can adapt;* June 2010

5   Poulton, P., et al: *Major limitations to achieving '4 per 1000' increases in soil organic carbon stock in temperate regions: evidence from experiments at Rothamsted Research, UK; Global* Change Biology, **24,** (6)

6   SAIN Digest 31st May 2016

7   Foresight (see ref.13, chapter 4)

8   Source – Lancrop Laboratories, Pocklington Industrial Estate, Pocklington, York, YO42 1DN

9   UK Parliament Environmental Audit Committee Report into Soil Health, 2nd June 2016: http//www.parliament.uk/business/committees/committeesa-z/commons-select/environmental-audit-committee/news-parliament-2015/soil-health-report-published-16-17

**Chapter 6 Research and Technology**

1   Carson, R., *Silent Spring;* Houghton Mifflin Company, (1962), ISBN 13-978 061824-9060

2   Report of debate in European Parliament; euractiv.com/section/agriculture-food/news/scientists-urge-action-against-insect-decline 11th November 2017. *Prof. Hans de Kroon*

3   SAIN notes February 2016: *China research highlights countries' excess use of antibiotics;* (Reuters, 22/02/2016) and State backed news website ThePaper.cn

4   Gellband, H., et al: *The State of the World's Antibiotics, 2015: Centre for Disease Dynamics, Economics and Policy (CCDEP), Washington D.C.* http//www.ccdep.org

5   AU 2003 *The Maputo Declaration on Agriculture and Food Security;* The African Union, http//www.nepad.org

6   Beintema, N., Stads, G.J., *Taking stock of National Agricultural R & D capacity in Africa south of the Sahara:* ASTI Synthesis Report, November 2014, http//www.asti.cgiar.org

7   Foresight (ibid. 13, chapter 4)

8   Godfray, H.C.J., et al: *The Future of the Global Food System:* Philosophical Transactions of the Royal Society **B** (2010), **365**, 2769-2777: doi:10.1098/rstb.2010.0180

9   http//www.cap2020,leep.eu/2014/12/1/food-security-a-motivating-force-for-useful-policy-change?s=1&selected=latest

10  Farmers Weekly, 7th November 2017

11  Muller, et al: *Strategies for feeding the world more sustainably with organic agriculture:* 2017, on www.fcrn.co.uk

12  Balmford, A., et al: *The environmental costs and benefits of high yield farming:* Nature Sustainability, **1,** 477-485, (2018)

13  Smil, V.,: *Nitrogen Cycle and World Food Production:* World Agriculture, (2011), Vol.2 no.1, pp 9-13

14  *European Nitrogen Assessment, 2011:* edited by Sutton, Mark, A., Summary for Policymakers, para. 52, p.xxxi, European Science Foundation, http//www.nine.esf.org: ISBN 978-1107-06126, Cambridge University Press

15  Westhoek, H., et al: (2015): *Nitrogen on the table: the influence of food choices on nitrogen emissions and the European environment: European Nitrogen Assessment special report on nitrogen and food:* Centre for Ecology and Hydrology, Edinburgh, UK

16  Catulle, M., et al, published in *Journal of Agriculture and Food Chemistry* as reported in *The Economist,* March 3rd, 2018

17  NIAB *Landmark Magazine,* May 2016, Article by Bill Clark

18  NIAB *Environment notes* prepared by AERU, University of Hertfordshire, November 2017

19  Beddington, J., *personal communication*

20  FAO Symposium on genetic manipulation as used in agriculture: FAO, Rome, February 2016

21  Juma, C., *The New Harvest: Agricultural Innovation in Africa,* (2011), Oxford University Press

REFERENCES

22. Montpelier Panel, December 2014: *No ordinary matter: conserving, restoring and enhancing Africa's soils*

23 Sebastian, Kate, (editor): *IFPRI, Atlas of African Agricultural Research and Development: revealing agriculture's place in Africa: (2014)*, http//www.ifpri.org

24 Juma, C., (ibid. 21)

25 FAO Commission on Genetic Resources for Food and Agriculture: *the state of the world's biodiversity for food and agriculture*, (2019)

26 World Bank Development Report, 2010: *Development and Climate Change: World Bank, Washington D.C.* http//openknowledge.worldbank.org/handle/10986/4387: License: CC BY 3.OIGO

27 Buffett, Howard, G., President of the Howard G. Buffett Foundation: *World Food Prize keynote address,* Des Moines, Iowa, 10th December 2011

28 Montpelier Panel (*ibid.* 22)

29 SAIN Policy Brief no. 60, December 2017

30 Fischer, A., et al: *Crop yields and global food security: will yield increase continue* to feed the world?: (2014), Australian Centre for International Agricultural Research; Grains Research and Development Corporation, Australian Government

31 Global Harvest Initiative: 2014 GAP Report: *Global revolutions in agriculture: the challenge and promise of 2050*

32 SAIN Working Paper no. 1, February 2018: *Agricultural development in China – environmental impacts, sustainability issues and policy impacts, assessed through China-UK projects under SAIN, 2008–17*

33 Rozelle, Scott, *Feeding China:* National Geographic Magazine, February 2018

**Chapter 7 Environment**

1 UK Partnership of 53 organisations including conservation charities, recording schemes and research organisations: *The State of Nature 2016:* http//www.rspb.org.uk/.../state-of-nature/state-of-nature-report2016.pdf

2 WWF International, *Living Planet Report 2016: risks and resilience in a new era.*

3 State of the World's Plants: Royal Botanic Gardens, Kew, http//www.stateofthe-worldsplants.com/2016

4 Chelsea Harvey, The Washington Post, Energy and the Environment: report on *The last frontiers of wilderness:Tracking lossesof intact forest landscapes from 2000 to 2013, published in Science Advances, January 2017*

5 World Economic Forum, *The Global Risks Report 2018*, http//www.reports.weforum.org/global-risks-2018

6 *Ibid.* 5

7 IPBES: *the IPBES assessment report on land degradation and restoration,* Montarella,

L., Scholes, R., and Brainish, A., (eds), Secretariat of the Intergovernmental Science-Policy Platform on Biodiversity and Ecosystem Services, Bonn, Germany,

8   United Nations Environment Programme (UNEP): *ibid.2, chapter 4*

9   *Ibid. 8*

10  *European Nitrogen Assessment: ibid.14, chapter 6*

11  http//www.theguardian.com/environment/2018/feb/16/dutch-cow-poo-overload-causes-an-environmental-stink?.org=1364&lvl=1004&ite=1105&lea=142040&cts=04par=1&trk=, article on Friday 16th February 2018 by Tom Levitt

12  Farmers Weekly, 2nd February, 2018, p.17 : Goves *'green' Brexit plan*

13  *UK Climate Change Risk Assessment 2017:* http//assets.publishing.service.gov.uk/.../climate-change-risk-assessment.2017.pdf

14  Buckwell: *ibid.9, chapter 6*

15  The Economics of Ecosystems and Biodiversity TEEB (2015); *TEEB for Agriculture & Food: an interim report:* United Nations Environment Programme, Geneva, Switzerland, www.img.teebweb.org

16  SAIN December 2016: report from Xinhua news agency, 29th August 2016: *China tops the world for having 70m ha. of planted forest*

17  *Policy Recommendations to the World Bank: Biosphere Smart Agriculture in a True Cost Economy:* published by Foundation Earth and Watershed Media (2015), http//consultations.worldbank.org/Data/hub/files/biosphere-smart-agriculture-in-a-true-cost-economy

18  Carney, M., *Breaking the tragedy of the horizon: climate change and financial stability,* a speech to Lloyds of London, 29th September 2015

19  Haldane, A., Speech at *Oxford China Business Forum,* Beijing, 9th September 2010

20  EU High-Level Expert Group on Sustainable Finance: *Financing a Sustainable European Economy: Final Report 2018,* http//e.c.europa.eu/info/sites/files/180131-sustainable-finance-final-report-en.pdf

21  Ian J. Bateman et al, *Bringing Ecosystem Services into Economic Decision Making: Land Use in the United Kingdom (2013):* Science **341,** 45, (2013), DOI: 10.1126/science.1234379

22  *TEEB for Agriculture and Food, Introductory note on valuation framework:* Writers Workshop, 9-10 May, Paris

**Chapter 8 Waste**

1   Waste Resources and Action Programme UK (WRAP): *Household food waste in the UK, 2015; Final Report, January 2017,* www.wrap.wrap-tbx-drupal-torchboxapps.com/sites/files/wrap/Household-food-waste-in-the-UK-2015-Report.pdf

2   Willerson, C., et al. (2015), *Quantity and quality of food losses along the Swiss potato*

supply chain: Stepwise investigation and the influence of quality standards on losses: Waste Management, DOI: 10.1016/j.wasman.2015.08.033

3  Bond, M., et al. (2013): *Food waste within global food systems: A Global Security Report*

4  Britton, E., et al. *Econometric modelling and household food waste: WRAP, January 2014,* www.wrap.org.uk/sites/files/wrap/Econometrics%20Report.pdf

5  Alexander, P., et al. (2017): *Losses, innefficiencies and waste in the global food system:* Agricultural Systems **153**, (2017), 190-200

6  Economist Intelligence Unit, *Food Sustainability Index (2017):* www.foodsustainability.eiu.com/wp-content/uploads/sites/34/2016/09/foodsustainabilityindex2017/GlobalExecutiveSummary.pdf

7  National Resources Defence Council (NRDC), (2017): *WASTED: How America is losing up to 40% of its food from farm to fork to landfill:* 2nd edition of NRDC's original report., www.nrdc.org.issues/food-waste

8  SAIN China Agri-Food Digest, December 2014, No. 24: *extracted from Xinhua news Agency, 04-12-2014*

9  Times of India, 30/03/2018: *India's share in world trade in agriculture is just two percent*

10 Chicago Council, 07/04/2016, *GAP's Financial Diaries with Smallholder Households,* www.thechicagocouncil.org.blog-entry/guest commentary

11 Chicago Council, 07/04/2016, *Tackling food waste along the supply chain,* www.thechicagocouncil.org.blog-entry/Isabel-do-Campo

12 Global Food Security Report, *ibid.3*

13 Akinwumi Adesina, *Africa could tackle Insecurity with Smart Agricultural Policies:* Wall Street journal, April 20th 2015

14 Committee on World Food Security (CFS), *Report of the 41st Session of the Committee on World food security,* Rome, October 13-18, 2014

15 www.champions123.org

16 The Rockerfeller Foundation, *Yieldwise Initiative:* www.rockerfellerfoundation.org/our-work/initiatives/yieldwise

17 A joint initiative by UNEP,FAO and other partners – a global campaign to change the culture of food waste, *Think, Eat, Save initiative:* www.thinkeatsave.org:

18 FAO, IFPRI and other partners, *Technical Platform on the measurement and reduction of food loss and waste:* ensures information sharing; builds on, and complements existing initiatives and research programmes

19 A partnership between UNEP, WRAP, wbcsd, fusion, the consumer goods forum and World Resources Institute (WRI), *Food Loss and Waste Accounting and Reporting Standard: Version 1.0, Food Loss + Waste Protocol.* www.wri.org/sites/default/files/REP_FLW_Standard.pdf

**Chapter 9 Diet and Health**

1  World Health Organisation (WHO): *Child obesity surveillance initiative:* www.euro.int/en/health-topics/noncommunicable-diseases/...southern-european-countries-have-highest-rates-of-chlidhood-obesity

2  *Precarious Lives: Food, work and acre after the Global food crisis,* Sept. 2016: Institute for Development Studies and Oxfam: www.ids.ac.uk/.../precarious-lives-food-work-and-care-after-the-global-food-crisis

3  F. Imamura et al.: *Dietary quality among men and women in 187 countries in 1990 and 2010: a systematic analysis,* on behalf of the Global Burden of Diseases Nutrition and Chronic Diseases Expert Group (NutriCoDE): Lancet Global Health, 2015, **3**, (3): DOI:10.1016/52214-109X(14)70381-X

4  Keats, S., Wiggins, S., *Future Diets – implications for agriculture and food prices:* Overseas Development Institute (odi), London

5  Scientific Report of the 2015 Dietary Guidelines Advisory Committee: *US Dietary Guidelines Report, 2015,* http//health.gov.dietaryguidelines/2015-scientific-report/

6  Washington Post, 12/10/2017: *Why Chicago's soda tax fizzled after two months – and what it means for the anti-soda movement*

7  www.fcrn.org.uk/print/research-library/world-health-organisation-says-sugary-soft-drinks-should-be-taxed-worldwide-address

8  WHO *ibid.*1

9  Mason, P., Lang, T., *Sustainable Diets: how ecological nutrition can transform consumption and the food system:* Routledge, Earthscan, 2017: ISBN978-0-415-744-70-6

10  Health effects of Overweight and Obesity in 195 countries over 25 years: www.nejm.org.doi/full/10.1056/NEJMoa1614362

11  Global Panel on Agriculture and Food Systems, 2016: *Foresight report on Food Systems and Diets: Facing the Challenge of the 21st century,* London, UK, www.glopan.org/news/foresight-report-food-systems-and-diets

12  Washington Post, 21/05/2017: *Report on International Food Information Council Foundation, 12th Annual Food and Health Survey, 2017*

13  FAO: www.foodsource.org.uk/book/export/html/88 (section 10.1.1)

14  Mason and Lang: ibid.9

15  British Dietetic Association launches new Sustainable Diets Policy Statement, 25/01/2018, www.bda.uk.com/news/view?id=1944x%5BO%5D=news/list

16  World Economic Forum White Paper, 2018: *Meat: The future: time for a protein portfolio to meet tomorrow's demand, January 2018,* www3.weforum.org/.../White Paper Meat the Future Time Protein Portfolio Meet Tomorrows Demand

17  Ibid.16

18  www.fcrn.org.uk/research-library/protein-shift-will-europeans-change-their-diet

19  www.euractiv.com/section/climate-environment/news/friclimate-change-means-meat-taxes-are-increasingly-likely

20  World Economic Forum, *ibid.16*

21  *For instance:* John Hopkins Centre for a livable future: *The importance of reducing animal product consumption and wasted food in mitigating catastrophic climate change:* sourced from fcrn.co.uk/research-library

22  *and:* Chatham House, London: *Changing Climate, Changing Diets: pathways to lower meat consumption:* sourced from fcrn.co.uk/research-library

23  Wiley Online Library, *Global environment costs of China's thirst for milk-Bai-2018:* Global Change Biology: www.onlinelibrary.wiley.com/doi/abs/10.1111/gcb.14047?org=1364&ite=1606&lea=142040&ctr=0tpar=1&trk=&

24  UK Committee on Climate Change, *ibid.5*, Chapter 2

25  Myers, S., *Carbon dioxide may rob crops of nutrition leaving millions at risk:* Harvard School of Public Health, 2017: www.npr.org/sections/thesalt/2017/08/02/540650904/carbon-dioxide-may-rob-crops-of-nutrition-leaving-millions-at-risk

26  UN Sustainable Goals, 2015: www.sustainabledevelopment.un.org/sdg2

27  Tschirley, D., et al. *The rise of a middle class in East and Southern Africa – implications for a food system transformation:* UNU-WIDER working paper, 2014/119

28  Foresight, *ibid.11*

**Chapter 10 Farmers**

1  TEEB: *ibid.15, chapter 7*

2  As reported in *Euractiv* 11th July 2018

3  Farmer's Weekly, 7th October 2016, blog by Jessica McIsaac, *Emissions and wages challenges*

4  www.euractic.com, *02/10/2017, Agri-policy and the environment: seeking the right balance*

5  www.princescountrysidefund.org.uk/research/the-cash-flow-crisis-in-farming

6  Farmer's Weekly, 06/05/2016, *Comment, p.6*

7  House of Lords: *Responding to price volatility – creating a more resilient agricultural sector:* European Union Committee, www.publications.parliament.uk/pa/ld201516/ldselect/ideucomm/146/14603htm

8  De Schutter, O., www.foreignpolicy.com/2015//07/20/starving-for-answers-food-water-united-nations

9  www.theguardian.com/sustainable-business/food-blog/10-things-to-know-global-food-system

10 Institute for Agriculture and Trade (IATP): *Emissions Impossible*, www.iatp.org/emissions-impossible

11 Farmer's Weekly, 08/10.2016, *News: Green subsidy now intensifies:* author, Philip Case

12 Bill Clark (NIAB), personal communication

13 www.landesa.org/resources/property-not-poverty

14 *Ibid.14/resources/anatomy-of-a-tiger*

15 SAIN, China Agri-food News Digest, 27, March 2015

16 Yiyun Wu, et al. (PNAS, 2018), *Policy distortions, farm size and the overuse of farm chemicals in China,* www.pnas.org.cgi.doi/10.1073/pnas1806645145: published by PNAS by N-circle project team (funded by BBSRC- NERC Newton fund)

17 The Chicago Council: www.thechicagocouncil.org.blog/global-food-for-thought/falter...ntent=text&org=1364&lvl=100&ite-1910&lea=142040&ctr=0&par=18=trk=

18 The Economist, July 14th 2018: *Agriculture in India: Slim pickings*

19 New York Times, 5th March 2015: www.nytimes.com/2015/03/05/world/asia/poor-state-of-Indias-subsidies, html?ref=topics&r=2

20 The Economist, *ibid.19*

21 Byerlee, D., et al, Food Policy no 31, (2006), 275-287: *Managing food price risks and instability in a liberalising market environment: Overview and policy options*

22 www.africanarguments.org/2015/10/07/beware-the-green-revolution

23 African Centre for Biodiversity, Farm Input Subsidy Programmes (FISP's): *A benefit for, or a betrayal of SADC's small scale farmers?*, accessed from www.fcrn.org.uk/research-library/far-input-subsidy-programmes-benefitting-or-betraying

24 Greatrex, H., et al. (2015), *Scaling up Index Insurance for Smallholder farmers: Recent eveidence and insights:* CAFS Report no. 15, Copenhagen: CGIAR Research Program on Climate Change, Agriculture and Food Security (CCAFS), www.ccafs.org

25 The Guardian, Food Hub from Guardian Sustainable Business, 30/09/2014, www.theguardian.com/sustainable-business/food-blog/2014/sep/...insurance-could-protect-cattle-herders-in-Africa-from-drought

26 Technical Centre for Agriculture and Rural Cooperation ACP-EU: *Policy pointers, Agricultural Extension, a time for a change: Linking knowledge to policy and action for food and livelihoods, ISSN 2212-6333 (conference report)*

27 Page, H., August 2013, *Global Governance and Food Security as a Global Public Good,* Center on International Cooperation, New York University

28 *Ibid.28*, paragraph 83

29  *Ibid.28*, paragraph 102

30  FAO: The State of Agriculture, 2012: *investing in agriculture for a better future*, ISBN 978-92-5-107317-9

**Chapter 11 Government and Society**

1   *Ibid.8,* chapter 10

2   Harrington, L.J., et al (2018), *How uneven are changes to impact relevant climate hazards in a 1.5⁰C world and beyond?*, Geophysical Research Letters, **45**, (13), 6672–6680

3   The Economist, 4th August 2018, *The Black Hole of Coal, pp.16–18*

4   The Economist, 25th May 2019, *Not-so-cold-comfort, p.89*

5   Mazzucato, M., (2015, 2018), *The Entrepreneurial State – debunking public vs private myths*, ISBN 978-0-141-98610, *p.152*

6   Suchul, Kang, Elfatih, A.B. Eltahire, *North China Plain threatened by deadly heat-waves due to climate change and irrigation*, Nature Communications, **9**, article no. 2894 (2018)

7   World Economic Forum 2017, *Global Risk Review*, http//wef.ch/risks2017

8   Von Braun, J., Birner, R., *Designing Global Governance for Agricultural Development and Food and Nutrition Security*, Review of Development Economics, 2016, DOI: 10.1111/rode.12261, John Wiley and Sons

9   *Ibid. 7*

10  Marsh, J., *Weak International institutions prevent the full benefit of science based inno-vation being secured for consumers and the environment*, World Agriculture, Vol.5, no.1 (2014)

11  UNCTAD/TDR/2014, United Nations Trade and Development Report, 2014, Over-view, New York and Geneva, www.unctad.org/en/Publications-Library/tdr2014overview_en.pdf

12  *Ibid.10, (p.15)*

13  *Ibid.10 (p21)*

14  Overseas Development Institute, *www.odi.org/comment/10385-hidden-heist…offshore-plunder-hurting-Africa,* 22nd April 2016

15  www.euractiv.com/sections/development-policy/swiss-leaks…icy&utm_medium-email&utm_term=0_babs50ea4c-f3f994718f-245626594

16  Galbraith, J.K., (1958), *The Affluent Society*, ISBN 978-0-395-92500-3

17  Stern, N., *The Economics of Climate Change: The Stern Review*, Cambridge University Press, 2007, ISBN 978-0-521-70080-1

18  *Ibid.16, (p.xv)*

19 Lawson, N., *An Appeal to Reason – a cool look at global warming*, 2009, ISBN 10-0715638416

20 Cowan, T., *Stubborn Attachments – a vision for a society of free, prosperous and responsible individuals*, Stripe Press, 2018, ISBN 978-1-7322651-3-4

21 *Ibid.19, (p.68)*

22 Jackson, T., 2010,2017, *Prosperity without growth: foundations for the economy of tomorrow*, Earthscan, 2010, ISBN 978-1-138-93541

23 *Ibid.21, (p.163)*

24 The Economist, 30th April 2016, *The trouble with GDP, pp.23-26*

25 www.theguardian.com/news/datablog/2012/may/24/robert-kennedy-gdp

26 www.theguardian.com/commentisfree/2018/may15/price-natural-world-destruction-natural-capital

27 www.oxfordmartin.ox.ac.uk/opinion/view/408?utm_source=2&utm_medium=emails&utm_term=0_7b3caf5065-301ad9c4c4-232512829

28 TEEB: *ibid.15, chapter 7*

29 Tyndall Centre for Climate Change, 2016, accessed at www.fcrn.org/research-library/global-challenges-require-cross-cutting-solutions-bringing-together-water-energy

30 Daily Telegraph, 27th October 2015, Bootle, R., *Bright future for Africa will hinge on good governance*

31 Overseas Development Institute, *Shaping policy for development: The political economy of agricultural policy processes in Africa*, 24th September, 2014, London

32 Galbraith, J.K., (1983), *The Anatomy of Power*, ISBN 10-024-1111-617

33 Mazzucato, M., *ibid.4*

34 Hasegawa, T., et al, *Risk of increased food insecurity under stringent global climate change mitigation policy*, Nature Climate Change, **8**, 699-703 (2018)

35 The Economist, 18th August 2018, *When the levy breaks*, (p.62)

36 Dobbs, R., et al, *Overcoming Obesity: an initial economic analysis*, McKinsey Global Institute, November 2014

37 Mason and Lang: *ibid.6, chapter 9*

38 Godfray, C.J., et al, *Meat consumption, health and the environment*, Science, **361**, 243, (2018)

39 *Ibid.10,* chapter 10

40 Daily Telegraph, 29th January, 2018, *Business Telegraph*

41 The Economist, 11th August, 2018, *Choosing Plan B*

## Chapter 12 Problems and Solutions 1?

1  The Times, 13th October 2018, Max Hastings Comment, *We're in a dark age when hearts rule minds*

2  Washington Post: www.washingtonpost.com/opinions/its-time-to-look-at-the... 99_story.html/utm_tem=a76da2ab02db&wpisrc=nl_headlines&wpmm=1

3  Fernbach, P.M. et al, *Extreme opponents of genetically modified foods knoe the least but think they know the most,* Nature Human Behaviour, **3**, 251-256, (2019)

4  *For example:* Mayer, C., *Prosperity: Better business makes the greater good,* Oxford University Press, 2018, ISBN: 978-01-9882-400-8

5  *For example:* Hart, O., Zingales, L., *Companies should maximise shareholder welfare, not market value,* Journal of Law, Finance and Accounting, **2**, 247-274, (2017)

6  Foresight, *ibid.2, Chapter 1*

7  Global Food Security Programme, *A Food Systems Approach to Policy for Health and Sustainability,* September 2018, www.foodsecurity.ac.uk

8  Searchinger, T., et al, *Creating a sustainable food future – a menu of solutions to feed nearly 10 billion people by 2050,* World Resources Institute, in partnership with World Bank, UN Environment, UNDP, CIRAD and INRA, December 2018

9  FAO (2016): *Plates, Pyramids, Planet: developments in national healthy and sustainable dietary guidelines: a state of play assessment,* FAO, Environmental Change Institute and The Oxford Martin Programme on the Future of Food, ISBN: 978-92-5-109222-4, (FAO and University of Oxford, 2016)

10  The Lancet: *Food in the Anthropocene: the EAT Lancet Commission on healthy diets from sustainable food systems,* www.thelancet.com/commissions/EAT

11  UK Parliament, House of Commons Environmental Audit Committee: *Sustainable Seas,* 2018, www.publications.parliament.uk, published 17th January 2019

12  *Ibid.11*

13  The Economist, May 25th 2019, *Threatened Wetlands – Save the Swamp, p.42*

14  Global Risks Report 2018, *ibid.5, Chapter 7*

15  The Economist, November 24th 2018, *The Power of Fish, p.36*

16  Euractiv, 7th January 2019, *Why too many EU vessels still chase too few fish,* www.euractiv.com

17  Hilborne, R., *Moving to sustainability by learning from successful fisheries,* Royal Swedish Academy of Science, 2007, Vol. **36**, no. 4, June 2007

18  *Ibid.14*

19  www.npr.org/sections/thesalt/2016/06/30/484015370/1-in-10-people-may-face-malnutrition-as-fish-catches-decline

20  As reported in the Times, 14th August 2018, from Nature Ecology & Evolution, **2**,

1334, (2018), Cisneros-Montemayor, A.M., et al, *Achieving sustainable and equitable fisheries requires nuanced policies, not silver bullets*

21  FAO: *the State of World Fisheries and Aquaculture, 2018 – meeting the sustainable development goals*, Rome, License CCBY-NC-SA 3.0 IGO

22  *Ibid.19*

23  FAO: *fisheries and Aquaculture Circular 1089*

24  *Ibid.19 (p.71)*

25  *Ibid.19 (p.42)*

## Chapter 13 Problems and Solutions 2?

1  Morland, P., *The Human Tide: How population shaped the modern world*, ISBN: 978-1473-675-13-1, (2019)

2  The Economist, 2nd February 2019, *A School for Small Families*, pp.59-61

3  www.un.org/development/.../2018-revision-of-world-urbanisation-prospects.html

4  The Times: Report 27th December 2018

5  Lancet EAT Commission: *ibid.11, chapter 12*

6  World Economic Forum 2019, *Options for the Livestock Sector in Developing and Emerging Economies to 2030 and Beyond*, prepared by ILRI for WEF

7  *Ibid. 6*

8  Buckwell: *ibid.9, chapter 6*

9  Gerhardt, C. Et al, *How will cultured meat and meat alternatives disrupt the agricultural and food industry?*, AT Kearney, 2019

10  The John Innes Centre Magazine, *Advances, Winter 2018/19*

11  www.ripe-illinois-edu/news/turbo-charged-photosynthesis-could-make-crops-grow-faster-while-using-fewer-nutrients

12  Foresight: *ibid.2, chapter 1*

13  Balmford, A., *ibid.12, chapter 6*

## Chapter 14 Problems and Solutions 3?

1  Dietz, S., *The economics of 1.5$^0$C climate change:* Lecture to Oxford Martin School, University of Oxford, 14th February 2019, available on U-Tube

2  Washington Post: www.washingtonpost.com.world.europe/Frances-protesters...e7_story.html/?utm_term=82b6df9d4496wpisrc+nl_headlines&wpmm=1

3  Speech to delegates of the World Economic Forum, Davos, January 2019

4  Dietz, S., *ibid.1*

5  *Ibid.*

6  The Economist, 9th February, 2019, *Brave New Deal*
7  The Times, reporting on comments by Prof. Dame Sally Davies, 2nd and 21st December 2018
8  http://journals.plos.org/plosone/article?id=10,1371/journal.pone.0204139
9  Global Food Security Programme, *ibid. 8*, chapter 12
10 The Times, 7th January 2019, Paul Johnson (Director Institute for Fiscal Studies): *The need for independent thinking in analysis is greater than eve*
11 The Economist, February 9th 2019, *Crude Awakening*
12 Washington Post, 8th January 2019
13 *Ibid.8*
14 Lancet EAT Commission: ibid.5, chapter 13

**Chapter 15 Morality**
1  UN Global Environment Conference, 8th November 1989: available at the Thatcher Foundation website
2  As quoted by Jesse Norman in his biography of Adam Smith: *Adam Smith – what he thought and why it matters*, Allen Lane, 2018, ISBN: 978-0-241-32849-1
3  The Times, December 2018110

# Biographical Note

Philip Richardson is a retired Norfolk farmer with an interest in the future of food and farming, and how farming worldwide may have to change over the first half of the twenty first century in response to climate change and other massive global challenges. He combines his practical experience as a farmer and the knowledge gained through extensive world travel with summaries of recent academic studies to highlight problems and potential solutions. Having spent much of his working life combining farming with agricultural 'politics' he is able to comment on the hard decisions world leaders must take to address change quickly enough and on an unprecedented scale.

Following his retirement from active business, Philip studied for a Masters degree in International Development and Climate Change. Together with his knowledge of agricultural research and technology following many years as Chair of a farmer owned research centre, and similar experience addressing some of the environmental issues associated with modern farming practice in the UK, he has written a book which should appeal to interested non-academic readers and decision makers, but which also points those who wish to examine subjects in more depth to appropriate sources of information.

Lightning Source UK Ltd.
Milton Keynes UK
UKHW020810260420
362197UK00007B/633